Cultural Conceptions
and
Mental Illness

Cultural Conceptions and Mental Illness

A Comparison of Germany and America

John Marshall Townsend

The University of Chicago Press

Chicago and London

JOHN MARSHALL TOWNSEND is Associate
Professor of Anthropology
at Syracuse University.

The University of Chicago Press, Chicago 60637
The University of Chicago Press, Ltd., London

©1978 by The University of Chicago
All rights reserved. Published 1978
Printed in the United States of America

82 81 80 79 78   9 8 7 6 5 4 3 2 1

Library of Congress Cataloging in Publication Data

Townsend, John Marshall
    Cultural conceptions and mental illness.

    Bibliography: p.
    Includes index.
    1. Psychiatry, Transcultural—Germany, West.
2. Psychiatry, Transcultural—United States.
3. Psychology, Pathological—Etiology.
4. Social role.   5. Mental illness—Public
opinion.   I. Title.
RC455.4.E8T68   616.8'9   77–22342
ISBN 0–226–81098–4

For Tarlton and Virgie
and
Jim Bokey

Contents

Contents

Acknowledgments

The investigation reported in this book was supported, in part, by Public Health Service Research Training Grant 1 To 1 MH 11616–01A1 and Fellowship 1 F 1 MH 40306–01A1 from the National Institute of Mental Health. Aid was also provided by faculty research grants from the University of Montana, Missoula, and from Syracuse University.

Parts of the text have appeared previously in articles: "Cultural Conceptions and Mental Illness," *Journal of Nervous and Mental Disease* 160 (July, 1975): 409–21 (parts of chapters 2 and 3); "Cultural Conceptions, Mental Disorders, and Social Roles," *American Sociological Review* 40 (December, 1975): 739–52 (parts of chapters 1 and 2); "Self-Concept and the Institutionalization of Mental Patients," *Journal of Health and Social Behavior* 17 (September, 1976): 263–71 (parts of chapter 3); "Cultural Conceptions and the Role of the Psychiatrist in Germany and America," *International Journal of Social Psychiatry* (in press) (parts of chapter 1). I am grateful to these journals for permission to republish these materials.

I wish to thank the following colleagues for reading earlier versions of the manuscript and offering their comments: Robert Edgerton, William Madsen, Tamotsu Shibutani, Charles Erasmus, Thomas Harding, Charles McClintock, Kay Valentine, and John S. Strauss, M.D.

The cooperation of the staffs in the target hospitals was also vital, and I would like to thank the following persons in this regard: Professor H. J. Bochnik, Professor Caspar Kuhlenkampf, the late Professor S. Wieser, George Plagens, M.D., and Werner Ziegler, M.D.

Invaluable aid in data collection was provided by Ann

Hanson, M.S.W., Peter Crell, M.D., and Frank Johnson, M.D.

I would also like to acknowledge the influence of the women in my life, Cynthia and Care. Without them the book would probably have been completed much sooner, but it would certainly have lost in "depth" and "insight."

Finally, I wish to express my deep appreciation to the approximately 200 mental patients in Germany and America who participated in the study. They really provided the essence of the study, and it is they, I hope, who will benefit most from it.

Introduction

In the past two decades a heated debate has developed over the nature of mental disorders. Traditionally, clinicians have insisted that mental disorders are diseases and should be treated as such. A number of authors have challenged this view. They argue that what is termed "mental illness" actually consists of deviant social roles. In their view, these deviant social roles are culturally conditioned by the same order of forces as "normal" roles. This approach has been termed variously the "sociological model" (Murphy 1976) or "cultural determinism" (Edgerton 1966). In this book, this approach will be termed "the social-role approach" and will encompass all of those authors who have, with varying emphases, argued that much of the behavior now termed "mental illness" is better understood as culturally conditioned social roles (Benedict 1934; Szasz 1960, 1963, 1970; Goffman 1961; Laing and Esterson 1964; Sarbin 1969; Scheff 1966; Braginsky et al., 1969; Rosenhan 1973). I use "role" in the sense of Linton's classic distinction between status and role (1936: 113–14). A status is a collection of rights and duties. *Role* represents the dynamic aspect of a status. That is, when a person is socially assigned to a status and exercises its rights and duties, he is performing a role. Status and role are thus only theoretically separable. This definition, of course, implies a certain predictability. For a social role to exist, there must be some agreement on what rights and duties constitute its status. If, for example, a butcher begins to act like a policeman, he breaches role expectations because he is exercising rights and duties which do not belong to his socially assigned status. His behavior is thus no longer predictable from his status, and people will find it upsetting. By the term "mental disorder" (or "illness") I refer generally to any of the conditions described in the American Psychiatric Association's *Diagnostic and Statistical Manual* (1968). The discussion in this work, however, does tend to focus on the major psychoses (affective psychoses and schizophrenia). Chapter 5 discusses whether mental disorders are best described as "diseases" or "social roles."[1]

The social-role approach to mental disorders has been challenged on various grounds, including lack of empirical evidence and internal inconsistencies (Gove 1975 a, b; Chauncey 1975). Recently, Murphy (1976) has argued that cross-cultural evidence on mental disorders does not support the social-role approach. The social-role approach implies that a broad cross-cultural variation in symptoms should exist because, insofar as symptoms are social roles, they should be specific to particular cultural statuses. On the other hand, if mental disorders are really diseases (like tuberculosis or smallpox), then the symptoms should show minimal cross-cultural variation. Traditional clinicians claim that the signs and symptoms of mental disorders (particularly schizophrenia) are universal and that societal reactions to these symptoms are similar throughout the world. They therefore conclude that social-role advocates have grossly overestimated the cross-cultural variation of symptoms and have therefore greatly overstated the power of social-role theory to explain mental illness. This is the stance taken by several authors of cross-cultural studies of mental disorders (e.g., Murphy 1976; Forster 1962; Kiev 1972; Zung, 1969; Ciba Foundation Symposium 1965). In the present discussion, this approach will be termed "clinical universalism" (Edgerton 1966).

The primary purpose of this book is to explore empirically two contemporary theories of the social-role school. The first of these is Thomas Scheff's thesis (1966) that popular stereotypes of insanity act as a guideline for behavior in shaping the symptoms of mental illness. The second is Erving Goffman's theory that the requirements of institutional life are primary shapers of the behaviors associated with chronic mental illness (1961).

Although this study is primarily concerned with the social-role approach to mental disorders, it is not meant as a repudiation of the clinical viewpoint. Rather, this study explores two social-role theories of mental illness, using data from matched samples of German and American high-school students, mental patients, and mental-hospital staff. These data are analyzed in chapters 1–3. In chapters 4 and 5 I will argue that the impasse between the social-role and clinical-universalist positions is the product of a false dichotomy, and I will attempt to reconcile this dichotomy by utilizing a psychophysiological conception of "social role."

The social-role approach to mental disorders has its roots in the early work of culture and personality researchers and particularly in the work of Margaret Mead and Ruth Benedict. These authors established principles that have remained profoundly influential in contemporary psychiatric anthropology. We can summarize these principles as follows. First, behavior disorders vary cross-culturally because they are molded by the particular stresses and strains within a given society. Second, virtually no act is inherently abnormal; cultural context and mores define what is "normal" or "abnormal." Ruth Benedict was probably the first to formulate these principles clearly (1934:75). She argued that virtually any behavior could be normal in a society. If trance is valued in a society, people will have supernormal experiences; if homosexuality is considered normal for males of certain ages, males of that age will be homosexual; if a society encourages acquisitiveness (as does ours), people will amass property. The vast majority of the populace in any society conform to their society's rules, roles, and definitions, although these same rules, roles, and definitions may be considered aberrant in other societies (Benedict 1934:75).

For Benedict, then, the normality of any behavior could only be defined relative to a particular culture. She did not deny the possibility of universal criteria for normality-abnormality, but she felt that, with adequate cross-cultural research (Benedict 1934:79), this universal definition of abnormality would probably be quite unlike our "culturally conditioned, highly elaborated" psychoses, schizophrenia and manic depression. This relativistic approach has retained fundamental significance in the work of contemporary researchers. For example, Schooler and Caudill (1964) utilized it in comparing urban Japanese and American schizophrenics. Their results indicated that schizophrenic symptoms tend to follow the path of "most resistance": the incidence of symptoms tends to be greater in areas of behavior that are particularly stressed by the cultures.

Virtually the same perspective underlies Anthony Wallace's study (1972) of Arctic hysteria, except that this time we find a new dimension introduced: not only do symptoms follow cultural patterns of stress, but a culture's conceptions or theories about that illness profoundly shape its course. Wallace believes that the Eskimo disease *pibloktoq* (Arctic hysteria) has as its root cause hypocalcemia (calcium deficiency), but Eskimos' expectations concerning the disorder act upon the behavior of an afflicted person in such a way as to produce a definite pattern. The Eskimos believe that an afflicted person passes through five definite stages. Although the person's actual behavior may not exactly conform to their theory, his behavior is definitely affected by it. The folk model of the disorder thus tends to regularize what otherwise might be highly variable behavior.

The idea that a culture's theories or conceptions of a disorder greatly affect its symptoms and course has been applied in a variety of exotic settings (e.g., Fogelson 1965; Newman 1964), but only recently has it been applied systematically to mental illness in industrial societies. Scheff (1966) has proposed that the conceptions (or stereotypes) of insanity profoundly shape symptomatology. He sees these popular conceptions operating as a sort of folk model that structures sick roles in our society much as folk models do in primitive societies. Although he never explicitly uses the term "folk model," Scheff, in developing his argument, makes direct use of anthropological literature on folk models (e.g., Wallace 1972; Fogelson 1965). The dynamics underlying Scheff's thesis are summarized in the following paragraph (Scheff 1966:82):

> In a crisis, when the deviance of an individual becomes a public issue, the traditional stereotype of insanity becomes the guiding imagery for action, both for those reacting to the deviant and, at times, for the deviant himself. When societal agents and persons around the deviant react to him uniformly

in terms of the traditional stereotypes of insanity, his amorphous and unstructured rule-breaking tends to crystallize in conformity to these expectations, thus becoming similar to the behavior of other deviants classified as mentally ill, and stable over time. The process of becoming uniform and stable is completed when the traditional imagery becomes a part of the deviant's orientation for guiding his own behavior.

Scheff has thus utilized what has been a traditional anthropological approach to mental disorders. Like Benedict, he emphasizes that normality/abnormality is defined by cultural mores and that behavior disorders vary with cultural conceptions and cultural stress.

Goffman's now classic study of asylums (1961) can also be viewed as an example of the social-role approach. Goffman argued that the mental hospital is the major determinant of the roles of chronic mental illness. In order to effect patient compliance with institutional needs, the hospital must bring the patient to accept its view of him. To do this often requires that the patient's view of himself be discredited. The ultimate effect of this process may be the institutionalization of the patient: the patient accepts the roles proffered by the institution and becomes locked into them. He becomes incapable of performing normal roles outside the institution. This, Goffman argues, is a major determinant of the behavior associated with chronic mental illness.

Chapters 1 and 2, below, present a test of Scheff's theory, using data from a comparison of Germany and America. Chapter 3 uses data from the same comparison (and other sources) to discuss Goffman's theory of institutionalization. Germany and America were chosen for the study both because their cultural similarities would limit the number of variables and thus make comparisons more useful and because previous studies had suggested that conceptions of mental illness differed significantly in the two countries (Nunnally 1961; Jaeckel and Wieser 1970).[2] In chapter 4 I will argue that although the major psychoses appear to be found universally, psychiatric labeling and treatment are, in part, cultural products. As such, they function as mechanisms of social control that can have damaging effects. The evidence for this view has evolved considerably in recent years. Originally, proponents of the social-role approach were either social scientists (Goffman 1961; Scheff 1966) or renegade psychiatrists (Szasz 1960; Laing 1967) whose arguments were generally more theoretical or phenomenological than empirical and statistical. Lately, however, numerous quantitative studies have appeared that support tenets of the social-role approach. These studies have come not from critics on the sidelines but from highly respected research psychiatrists and have appeared in the most prestigious psychiatric journals (e.g., Strauss and Carpenter 1972; Kendall et al. 1971; Carpenter et al. 1977). Chapter 4 seeks to demonstrate that the social-role thesis no longer arises solely from a dialectic between the psychiatric establishment and its critics but rather has become a matter of serious scientific debate within the psychiatric community.

In chapter 5 I attempt to bridge the gulf between the clinical-universalist and social-role schools by demonstrating that they continue to dichotomize between biology and learning and tend to utilize different populations to buttress their arguments. Utilizing a psychophysiological conception of "role," I reject this dichotomy and propose a synthesis of the two approaches.

For the reader's convenience, tables of statistical results are juxtaposed with their discussion in the text. Tables presenting bulkier supportive material (e.g., samples, questionnaire items) appear in the Appendix.

1 Popular and Professional Conceptions of Mental Illness in Germany and America

The social-role approach to mental disorders implies that a broad cross-cultural variation in symptoms should exist because, insofar as symptoms are social roles, they should be molded by particular cultural and behavioral contexts. In his analysis of mental disorders as social roles, Scheff has stated this explicitly (1966: 82–83):

> The idea that cultural stereotypes may stabilize residual rule-breaking and tend to produce uniformity in symptoms, is supported by cross-cultural studies of mental disorder. Although some observers insist there are underlying similarities, many agree that there are enormous differences in the manifest symptoms of stable mental disorder *between* societies, and great similarities *within* societies.

According to Scheff's theory, both before and after public labeling, the popular conceptions of mental illness, which have been learned and culturally reinforced since childhood, govern the expectations of the rule-breaker and of those around him and force his behavior into ever-increasing conformity with popular conceptions. The ultimate products of this process are the stereotyped roles of insanity.

Scheff's theory thus proposes that a culture's conceptions of mental disorders largely determine the process of defining someone as mentally ill. This definitional proc-

Parts of this chapter have appeared in my article "Cultural Conceptions, Mental Disorders, and Social Roles" in the *American Sociological Review 40* (December 1975): 739–52. Copyright © 1975 by the American Sociological Association. Reprinted by permission. Other parts are from my article "Cultural Conceptions and the Role of the Psychiatrist in Germany and America" which will appear in a forthcoming issue of the *International Journal of Social Psychiatry* and are reproduced here with the permission of the Avenue Publishing Company, London, England.

ess acts as a self-fulfilling prophecy, i.e., through inadvertent reinforcement from the social environment, the deviant's symptomatology ultimately comes to resemble the popular stereotypes. In this process, the stereotypes function as a "guideline for action," both for the deviant and for the laymen and professionals who react to him. Critical to any test of this theory, then, is information on the conceptions of mental disorders held by mental-health professionals and laymen.

It is an established fact that cultures vary in the way they view mental disorders (Benedict 1934; Linton 1956; Wallace 1972). Relating Scheff's theory to this cross-cultural variation, one would make the following predictions.

Proposition 1. Two different cultures with different conceptions of mental disorders will show differences in professional conceptions which correspond to the differences in the two cultures' popular conceptions.

Proposition 2. Mental patients' views of mental disorders in these two cultures will show differences which correspond to the differences in popular conceptions in the two cultures.

Proposition 3. Differences in symptom formation in these two cultures will correspond to the differences in the popular conceptions.

This chapter attempts to test proposition 1 in a comparison of Germany and America. Propositions 2 and 3 will be discussed in chapters 2 and 3.

Purpose

The purpose of this part of the investigation was to test the following hypotheses:

Hypothesis 1. Intercultural differences in popular and professional conceptions of mental disorders exceed intracultural differences. That is, professionals and laymen in each country should, in their conceptions of mental disorders, resemble each other more than they resemble their status equivalents in other countries.

Hypothesis 2. Regarding intercultural differences, the German and American professional groups should, as a result of professional socialization, resemble each other more than the German and American laymen resemble each other. Thus, based upon degree of expected similarities in conceptions of mental illness for the present samples, the following ranking of pairs is predicted: (1) intracultural differences (students versus professionals) approximately the same in either country (smallest differences); (2) German staff and American staff (greater differences); (3) German students and American students (greatest differences).

Methods

Samples

Students. To measure popular conceptions of mental illness in Germany and America, samples of high-school students were chosen in the areas of Seattle, Washington ($N = 728$) and Frankfurt am Main ($N = 552$). These samples were chosen to be representative of academic achievement levels and family income for high-school students in those urban areas.[1] In addition, the German sample was stratified according to the national percentages attending each type of high school in Germany: the Gymnasium (college preparatory); the Berufschule (professional occupational); and the Realschule (practical school). To some extent, this stratification correlates with socioeconomic class, for the lower classes tend to choose the practical and occupational schools, while the upper classes choose the college-preparatory schools. Because it is difficult in Germany to learn a respondent's approximate income, socioeconomic classification is generally accomplished according to occupation. Consequently, the two samples were matched, as closely as possible, on the basis of the father's (or principal breadwinner's) occupation. Table A in the Appendix indicates that the two student samples do generally approximate each other in terms of reported occupation for the principal income-earner. The reported family incomes of the American students are also consistent with their reported occupations: 18 percent of the American group had fathers or mothers who were officials or licensed professionals and 22 percent of the sample had incomes of over $17,000. Participation was made voluntary in each case, but returns were close to 100 percent once a school principal had decided to cooperate. More complete demographic characteristics of the two student samples are given in Table A.

Mental-hospital staff. To represent German professional conceptions of mental illness, samples of mental-hospital staff were chosen in Frankfurt, Köppern, Düsseldorf, Hannover, and Bremen. With the exception of the deep south, this selection offers a fairly complete regional representation of Germany. Since all prospective psychiatrists and neurologists must complete a residency term in a university clinic, and older, more traditional psychiatrists are often found in state mental hospitals, our sample, which included staff from both university clinics and state hospitals, offers a good representation of the "old guard" and the new German psychiatry. Cooperation was more easily obtained from the physicians, although the nursing staff did participate to some extent. A total of 102 questionnaires was obtained. Approximately 75 percent of the staff members who were contacted returned completed questionnaires.

The American-staff sample was chosen to match, as closely as possible, the German sample in terms of training, experience, and work setting. To obtain some geographic diversity, samples of hospital staff were obtained in Southern California and the Upstate New York area. More complete descriptions of the two staff samples are given in the Appendix, in Tables B and C. Examination of these tables reveals that, compared to the German sample, the American sample is slightly biased in favor of older physicians working in state hospitals. Regarding the present hypothesis, however, this is probably not a serious bias.[2] Participation was voluntary in both countries, and returns were approximately 75 percent in Germany and 80 percent in America. A total of 79 questionnaires was obtained in America.

Instruments

Nunnally's sixty-item Information Questionnaire (1961: 259–64) was utilized to assess conceptions of mental illness in Germany and America. This instrument was chosen in order to facilitate comparisons with Nunnally's data and because the questionnaire items had been derived from a broad spectrum of popular and professional conceptions and then subjected to a considerable array of validation procedures. The questionnaire consisted of sixty state- ments about mental health or illness followed by a seven- step "Disagree-Agree" scale. Thus a mean of 1.0 would indicate a group's total disagreement with an item, while a mean of 7.0 would indicate total agreement. The sixty-item questionnaire was translated with the aid of German col- leagues who were experienced in this type of research and who had some command of English. This group consisted of two sociologists, two psychiatrists, and one psycholo- gist. The translation was then submitted to a professional translator of German-English psychiatric literature. He acted as a consultant in editing the final version.[3]

In order to isolate conceptual dimensions common to both German and American groups, the results of the ques- tionnaire were factor-analyzed using the varimax rotation method and including all subjects in the study ($N = 1,461$). Mean factor scores were computed for the two staff groups and the two student groups, and these mean factor scores were subjected to four one-way analyses of variance.

Results: Factor 1

Three factors were derived whose Eigen values exceeded the traditional cutoff point (i.e., 1.0). The first factor had an Eigen value of 6.1 and explained 50 percent of the total variance. Factors 2 and 3 had Eigen values of 1.8 and 2.3 and respectively explained 15 and 19 percent of the total variance. Factor 1, then, was by far the strongest and most general factor. Two different themes emerged in factor 2; both themes relate to factor 1 and will thus be discussed in conjunction with that factor. Because the four groups re- sponded differently to the two themes in factor 2 (hence the low Eigen value and loadings), the factor was judged in- appropriate for statistical analysis. The results of this factor will therefore be presented descriptively. Factor 3 was more specific and will be discussed later. All questionnaire items with their means and standard deviations appear in Table E in the Appendix.

Factor 1: Environmental Forces and Personal Effort

Factor 1, environmental forces and personal effort, contained items that expressed broad, general conceptions of mental disorders. Items with high loading on factor 1 stress the importance of environmental factors in causing and curing mental disorders. Thus, according to the items comprised in this factor, providing a person with a vacation, a change of scene, or proper guidance or financial support can help prevent or cure mental disorders. Because mental disorders are transitory and mutable, a person must "try" to get well; he can "learn good emotional habits," should avoid worry, and should "read books on peace of mind." Table 1 depicts the items comprised in factor 1, with their loadings, means, and standard deviations.

TABLE 1   Responses of German and American Psychiatric Staff and Students to Questionnaire Items Regarding Environmental Causes of Mental Illness (Factor 1)

Item	Loading	Means				Standard Deviations
		AStu	GStu	AS	GS	
11. Mental illness can usually be helped by vacation or change of scene	.55	3.6	2.1	3.0	1.5	1.65
32. Helping the mentally ill person with his financial and social problems often improves his condition.	.49	4.7	3.1	5.6	4.6	1.78
55. Books on "peace of mind" prevent many people from developing nervous breakdowns.	.46	3.3	2.5	3.3	2.0	1.51
35. Early adulthood is more of a danger period for mental illness than later years.	.45	4.5	3.4	4.3	3.5	1.64
43. A poor diet often leads to feeblemindedness.	.43	3.7	2.8	2.8	1.7	1.74
29. The mentally ill have not received enough guidance from the im-	.42	4.0	3.4	4.2	2.7	1.80

TABLE 1 (continued)

Item	Loading	Means				Standard Deviations
		AStu	GStu	AS	GS	
portant people in their lives.						
45. Good emotional habits can be taught to children in school as easily as spelling can.	.40	4.1	3.2	3.6	2.1	1.91
27. Mental health is largely a matter of trying hard to control the emotions.	.39	3.9	3.1	3.1	2.4	1.79
40. Most mental disturbances in adults can be traced to emotional experiences in childhood.	.39	3.9	3.1	3.1	2.4	1.67
44. Emotionally upset persons are often found in important positions in business.	.39	4.4	3.4	4.5	3.2	1.61
42. A person can avoid worry by keeping busy.	.35	3.8	3.2	4.1	3.1	1.98
39. Women are more likely to develop mental disorders than men.	.35	3.4	2.7	3.0	2.1	1.64
5. People cannot maintain good mental health without the support of strong persons in their environment.	.33	4.2	3.2	3.3	2.7	1.95
21. The best way to mental health is avoiding morbid thoughts.	.30	3.4	3.1	3.2	1.8	1.85

AStu=American high-school students ($N=728$). GStu=German high-school students (555). AS=American mental-hospital staff ($N=79$). GS=German mental-hospital staff (102). A mean of 7 signifies total agreement; a mean of 1, total disagreement; a mean of 4, neutrality. See Appendix and text for description of samples and instrument.

As stated above, it was predicted that intercultural differences (i.e., staff versus staff and students versus students) would exceed intracultural differences (i.e., staff versus students within each country). It was further predicted that, because of professional socialization, the two staff groups would resemble each other more than the two student groups would. The results of four one-way analyses of variance tend to confirm both predictions. Table 2 presents the results of these comparisons and shows that, relative to the American groups, the German groups tended to reject the items in this factor. The intercultural differences were highly significant and tended to exceed the intracultural differences.

TABLE 2   Analysis of Variance of Factor 1 Scores for German and American Staff and Student Groups

	F	df	$P <$
Intracultural comparisons:			
American staff ($\bar{X} = .56$) and students ($\bar{X} = .51$)	0.45	1/805	—
German staff ($\bar{X} = -.84$) and students ($\bar{X} = -.60$)	8.66	1/652	.005
Intercultural comparisons:			
American and German staffs	171.87	1/179	.0001
American and German students	856.88	1/1278	.0001

American staff ($N = 79$); American students ($N = 728$); German staff ($N = 102$); German students ($N = 552$). See Appendix and text for description of samples and instrument.

It should be noted that the differences depicted in Table 2 are relative, not absolute. The range of the groups' means (simple means, not factor scores) on the items was quite narrow (1.5–5.9). This narrow range probably results from the ambiguity of questionnaire items. In constructing the questionnaire, Nunnally had eliminated all statements that elicited almost unanimous agreement or disagreement. This had the effect of eliminating most statements that were unequivocal. The statements that remained were therefore somewhat ambiguous; i.e., they could not be answered definitely on the basis of factual information. Subjects may have reacted to this ambiguity by indicating mild disagreement with an item (marking 2–4). Although they did not know whether a statement was absolutely false, they did know that it was too general to be *always* true. Despite the limited range of the means, differences between groups tended to be highly significant. Standard deviations tended to be small enough that a difference of only 0.40 between two groups' item means could be significant at the 0.001 level. Standard deviations ranged from 1.19 to 2.11.

Discussion: Factor 1

The results with regard to factor 1 directly support proposition 1 and hypothesis 1. Mental-health professionals in Germany and America resembled their lay compatriots in their conceptions of mental disorders more than they resembled each other. Americans, in contrast to Germans, tended to endorse the notions that mental disorders are environmentally induced and can be influenced by an individual's personal effort and willpower. Other sources tend to support these findings, and it behooves us to examine some of these now.

American Conceptions

To construct his questionnaire (an earlier version of the one used in this study), Nunnally (1961) gathered over 3,000 statements concerning mental illness from 22 public-information pamphlets, from professional publications, and from over 200 personal interviews with the general public. The statements were then made randomly positive or negative and were pretested for clarity and for bias in phrasing. A final pre-test on 350 persons was conducted to further refine the instrument. In a factor analysis of his final results, ten factors emerged. Three of these stressed the importance of environmental forces and personal effort in causing and curing mental illness. Thus, the results from a broad sampling of American conceptions clearly reflected these themes.

Moreover, Nunnally found that the public's responses to these factors did not deviate sharply from those of mental-health professionals. As in the present results, Nunnally's professional and public samples tended to parallel each other quite closely in their responses to the various factors (1961:23). Nunnally also found that public conceptions were not highly structured. Eigen values and factor loadings were low, and individuals' interview responses were uncertain and hesitant. Thus, no coherent "folk model" of mental illness appeared in Nunnally's results. This lack of structure in popular conceptions parallels a similar lack of structure among professionals. Among American specialists there is virtually no premise that goes unchallenged. For example, the notion of a strict dichotomy between illness and health is a matter of great debate in America. Some clinicians argue that health is always a matter of degree. Others, like the Germans, insist on a strict dichotomy: a person is either sick or healthy. Similarly, the nature of mental disease(s) and its causes are hotly disputed (Robbins 1966). Some researchers think that there are several diseases, each with its own particular cause. Others agree that there are multiple diseases but claim that each of these can spring from multivarious causes. Some clinicians prefer to think of "reaction patterns" rather than "mental diseases"; they tend to reduce all the syndromes to a single rubric like "mental disorder." Mental-health specialists from the social sciences are more inclined to reject the medical dichotomy of health/illness; they see instead a continuum of behavior, with mental illness merely representing extreme forms of normal reactions. Finally, there are a few authors who, though trained as psychiatrists, repudiate the notion of mental illness altogether. They claim that there is only deviant behavior and that the medical viewpoint is a somewhat crude and arbitrary device used to control that behavior (Laing 1967; Szasz 1960).

Thus, popular and professional conceptions in America tend to parallel each other in both their content and their lack of a coherent structure. In spite of this lack of structure, the evidence suggests that, seen as a whole, environmental causes are more important in American conceptions than in German. An examination of German conceptions supports this interpretation.

German Conceptions

The themes of environmental factors and personal effort did not emerge so strongly in a previous study of German conceptions. In a random sample of 150 adults in the city of Bremen, Jaeckel and Wieser (1970) found that the German layman tends to differentiate two separate orders of mental illness. *Gemütskrankheit* (emotional disturbance; melancholia) is a psychological disturbance caused by an external event. It is thus relative in nature, can be merely transitory, and is subject to therapeutic influence. *Geisteskrankheit* (mental illness; insanity), in contrast, is inherited, is therefore a result of a "physical disease process," runs a fixed course, and is not subject to therapeutic influence (1970:42). The authors point out that these popular conceptions closely parallel the dichotomous taxonomy of mainstream German psychiatry. Indeed, the similarity is striking.

Like its public, mainstream German psychiatry dichotomizes between mental disorders that are environmentally induced, and are therefore transitory and curable, and those that are endogenous, chronic, and determinate. These characteristics are clearly reflected in the following passages (Hoff and Arnold 1961:62):

> Present-day clinical psychiatry in Germany emerges most clearly in the formulations of Kurt Schneider: There is a strict separation between illness and health. Psychological abnormalities are either variants of human behavior or the result of organic illness. This empirical dualism must remain the heuristic guiding light. Every psychic abnormality can be classified by means of one of two categories: somatic-etiological or psychological-symptomatic. Thus, Schneider differentiated between those exogenous psychoses for which we cannot find any organic cause, and those which are organic in origin—endogenous psychoses.

The authors proceed to typify Schneider as the "logical successor to Kraepelin" and to quote Kolle, Schneider's colleague, as saying (1961:62):

> The indisputable fact that they [the endogenous psychoses] strike only the individual who is equipped with the appropriate hereditary endowment does not imprint upon them the stamp of "unavoidable," but bestows upon them the rank of an event as difficult to master as fate itself.

Thus, in addition to the present results, several other sources tend to support proposition 1 and hypothesis 1. Staff and public groups in Germany and America paralleled each other in their conceptions of mental illness, and intercultural differences between these groups tended to exceed intracultural differences. In their conceptions, the American groups stressed environmental factors and personal effort more than the Germans.

Results: Factor 2

Factor 2: Role of Psychiatrist

Table 3 presents the eight statements comprised in factor 2, the role of the psychiatrist, along with their loadings and group means. Two themes appear in these items. The first theme appears in the first four items (34, 13, 10, and 47) having the highest loadings on this factor (i.e., between .41 and .50). These portray the psychiatrist as a fatherly teacher vis-à-vis his patients. He trains them to control their emotions, recommends hobbies, and does not discuss their treatment with them. Item 15 continues this portrait of the therapist, but in this statement the psychiatrist's teaching function is one of leading the patient to "insight." The German staff consistently endorsed the first four items more strongly than the American staff but tended to reject item 15 relative to the American staff. The findings for the student groups are similar. The German students tended to endorse all of the items more strongly than the American students.

The second theme which seemed to emerge in this factor is that of willpower and self-control (items 27, 15, 21, and 33). According to items 21 and 27, in order to maintain good mental health, a person must make a personal effort to control his thoughts and emotions. But American groups endorsed these items more strongly than their German counterparts.

Item 33 proposes that mental patients usually make a good adjustment when they return to society. American groups agreed with this statement more than Germans. The connection between this item and the others will be established below. The range of the means for items in factor 2 was from 1.8 to 5.1, and the standard deviations ranged from 1.5 to 2.0.

Discussion: Factor 2

The four groups' responses to items in factor 2 may be quite consistent with their responses to questions com-

TABLE 3   Responses of German and American Staff and Students to Questionnaire Items Regarding the Role of the Psychiatrist (Factor 2)

Item	Loading	Means				Standard Deviations
		AStu	GStu	AS	GS	
34. The good psychiatrist acts like a father to his patients.	.50	4.6	5.1	3.4	4.0	1.77
13. The main job of the psychiatrist is to recommend hobbies and other ways for the mental patient to occupy his mind.	.47	3.4	3.8	2.2	2.5	1.97
10. Psychiatrists try to teach mental patients to hold in their strong emotions.	.43	2.9	4.0	2.4	3.6	1.97
47. When a person is recovering from a mental illness, it is best not to discuss the treatment that he has had.	.41	3.9	4.6	2.6	3.1	1.87
27. Mental health is largely a matter of trying hard to control the emotions.	.35	3.9	3.1	3.1	2.4	1.79
15. Psychiatrists try to show the mental patient where his ideas are incorrect.	.35	4.3	4.6	4.5	3.8	1.80
21. The best way to mental health is by avoiding morbid thoughts.	.32	3.4	3.1	3.2	1.8	1.85
33. Mental patients make a good adjustment to society when they are released.	.28	4.1	3.9	4.1	3.2	1.48

AStu = American high-school students ($N = 728$); GStu = German high-school students ($N = 555$); AS = American mental-hospital staff ($N = 79$); GS = German mental-hospital staff ($N = 102$). A mean of 7 signifies total agreement; a mean of 1, total disagreement; a mean of 4, neutrality. See text for description of samples and instrument.

prised in factor 1. To understand the connection, it is necessary to examine the items in factor 2 individually. The four items with loadings greater than .40 on this factor (the first four items in Table 3) concerned the role of the psychiatrist. According to these statements, the psychiatrist acts like a father to his patients, teaching them to control their emotions, recommending hobbies to occupy their minds, and not discussing their treatment with them. Examining simple group means for these four items, the German staff ($\bar{X} = 3.3$) and German students ($\bar{X} = 4.4$) tended to accept these propositions relative to the American staff ($\bar{X} = 2.6$) and American students ($\bar{X} = 3.7$). These findings are consistent with the sketch of German psychiatry presented above. If the patient's condition is genetic in origin, the psychiatrist in a sense acts first as a neurologist in diagnosing the patient and then assumes a fatherly, custodial role in training the patient to control himself and to occupy himself with useful activities. It is significant in this regard that, in Germany, neurology generally receives much more weight in the psychiatric curriculum than does training in psychotherapeutic techniques. Indeed, in order to receive such training, it is frequently necessary for the resident in psychiatry to go outside his program, to a psychoanalytic institute, to undergo a training analysis. Consistent with this neurological emphasis is the Germans' response to item 47: "When a person is recovering from a mental illness, it is best not to discuss the treatment that he has had." The American staff and student means on this item were 2.6 and 3.9, respectively. The German staff and student means were 3.1 and 4.6, respectively. The Germans' relative endorsement of this item seems to be explained by their relative rejection of psychotherapeutic principles. If one believes that mental illness springs from genetic causes, there is little point in discussing the patient's treatment with him or in leading him to gain insight into his problems.

There were four items with loadings between .28 and .35 on this factor (the last four items in Table 3). These items posited that avoiding morbid thoughts, controlling one's emotions, and concentrating on pleasant memories help prevent mental illness. The German staff ($\bar{X} = 2.8$) and German students ($\bar{X} = 3.7$) tended to reject these items compared to the American staff ($\bar{X} = 3.7$) and students ($\bar{X} = 3.9$). This tendency, of course, is the reverse of the groups' responses to the first four items, and this reversal helps explain why the two staff groups' overall factor means did not differ markedly from each other on this factor. The German staff's relative endorsement of the more highly loaded items was offset by its relative rejection of items with somewhat lower loadings. Moreover, it is clear from an examination of Table 3 that these two groups' responses to these items are consistent with their responses to factor 1. As noted above, the first four items depict the psychiatrist in a role consistent with a genetic orientation, which deemphasizes environmental factors in causing and curing mental disorders. The two German groups tended to endorse these items more strongly than the American groups. The second four items reflect the same themes found in factor 1: personal effort and environmental conditions are crucial to the preservation of mental health. To maintain good mental health, a person must work at controlling his emotions and preserving a positive frame of mind. The German staff tended to reject these items relative to the American staff, while the two student groups had virtually identical means for these items. Thus, when examined individually, the groups' responses to factor 2 are not inconsistent with their responses to factor 1. Examined in this way, these results also tend to support hypothesis 1.

Conceptions and National Character

In this section I will attempt to sketch some possible connections between American conceptions of mental illness and more general cultural values and orientations. I will not attempt to tie the questionnaire results to a discussion of German national character because the questionnaire is not fully representative of German conceptions. The reader will remember that questionnaire items were gleaned from diverse public-information materials and extensive personal interviews in the United States. The themes embodied in these items thus represent statements which Americans would (or did) make about mental health. They are not necessarily statements that Germans would make, and I believe that it is for this reason that the Germans, compared to the Americans, tended to reject many items. Comparing the questionnaire items with Jaeckel and Wieser's analysis (1970) of German conceptions, one finds almost no mention of endogenous causes in the American statements. Words like "endogenous," "constitutional," "heritable," and "organic" were frequent elements in the German public's conceptions of mental illness but were relatively absent from the American questionnaire.

If we assume, then, that the questionnaire is more representative of American conceptions, it makes more sense to discuss the results in terms of American character. This is not to imply that the traits to be discussed are uniquely American but rather that these traits are *more* characteristic of the United States than of Germany (and other countries). In chapter 2 we will examine research on mental patients that lends support to this interpretation. Extensive open-ended interviews were conducted with German and American mental patients. These interviews allowed subjects to formulate their conceptions of mental illness in their own terms. Analysis of the results revealed the same cultural differences as the results of factors 1 and 2. Although the two national groups overlapped, American patients tended to emphasize environmental causes, personal effort, and willpower, while German patients stressed biological causes and the determinate nature of mental illness.

At this juncture the reader should note that *all* mainstream European psychiatry is more "biological" and "genetic" than American. Scandinavian psychiatry, for example, is in this respect probably more like German than American psychiatry. I thus do not believe that the period of National Socialism in Germany is responsible in any important way for the biological orientation of contemporary German psychiatry, and I consequently eschew a discussion of this period in this book.

During this research I have found that the word "Germany" evokes stereotyped images of Nazis and of authoritarianism in the minds of many Americans (including academics who should know better). I believe that for many people this stereotype performs the same functions as other stereotypes of ethnic and stigmatized groups. As we shall see in chapter 2, these stereotypes, whether of ethnic minorities or the mentally ill, serve as "contrast conceptions." They allow the viewer to exorcise his own demons by projecting them onto an out-group, and they tend to establish boundaries on a particular behavioral trait. It is thus more soothing for many Americans to talk about a war and genocide perpetrated over thirty years ago by "them" than to acknowledge their own silence (and comfortable life) while over six million Southeast Asians were being killed. As Milgram's experiments (1965) on obedience have shown, it is not necessary to posit an "authoritarian character" to explain German obedience during the war. Good Americans are also obedient when they perceive authority as legitimate—obedient enough to give ostensibly lethal shocks to an old man with a heart condition (Milgram 1965). Accordingly, I feel that a discussion of National Socialism is no more relevant to the present topics than a discussion of slavery in America, America's involvement in the war in Southeast Asia, or the CIA's role in military coups around the world. Furthermore, as we shall see in chapter 4, it is America rather than Germany which more readily uses its mental-health system to control a large disadvantaged population. For what I consider reasonable discussions of German national character, I refer the reader to Lowie (1954) and Breitenstein (1968).

Studies of national character have always been the subject of considerable controversy in social science (Greenstein 1965; Lindesmith and Strauss 1950; Mead 1954), and a thorough treatment of this topic is, in any case, outside the scope of this discussion. Consequently, instead of attempting a detailed review of the literature, I will concentrate on isolating several points of agreement in some well-known works on American character. These points of agreement will then be compared to the themes embodied in factors 1 and 2. In chapter 4 I will discuss these themes' political implications.

Francis Hsu (1972) has described self-reliance as the "core value" of American society. According to this thesis, self-reliance underlies (and thus can explain) the apparent contradictions in American values: the militant insistence on equality and the facts of inequality; Christian love and religious bigotry; rugged individualism and slavish conformity; contempt for weakness and humanitarianism. According to Hsu, America lacks stable institutions (e.g., kinship ties) which confer identity and give the individual a secure place in society. The value on self-reliance demands that people must make it on their own, and so traditional sources of support must be renounced. This forces the individual to compete for his status and identity through achievement and material consumption. Those who are less successful are held responsible for their failure. The following paragraph summarizes this part of Hsu's argument (1972:250):

> American self-reliance is then not new. As a concept it is in fact well known and well understood ... Suffice it to say here that under this ideal every individual is his own master, in control of his own destiny, and will advance and regress in society only according to his own efforts. He may have good or bad breaks, but
>
>> Smile and the world smiles with you,
>> Cry, and you cry alone ...
>
> In American society the fear of dependence is so great that an individual who is not self-reliant is a misfit. "Dependent character" is a highly derogatory term, and a person so described is thought to be in need of psychiatric help.

Hsu's portrait is generally consistent with other studies of American culture. Margaret Mead, for example, in discussing male and female roles, argues that interpersonal relations in America become an arena for competition, status-seeking, and consumption. The relations themselves may be quite contentless; what counts is that having a particular kind of partner says something about a person's ability to compete and achieve. Like Hsu, Mead also notes that fear of failure and dependency is a powerful force in shaping American character (Mead 1968:268–320). Jules Henry's incisive dissection of American culture is similar. Henry (1963) argues that competition, lack of emotional involvement in their jobs, and the continual struggle for success cause many Americans to turn to their families for security and emotional support. This institution, however, is ill-prepared to meet such demands because it has been eroded by the same economic forces that produced the search for security. In his analysis, then, Henry stresses the same American traits and values as the previous authors: emphasis on self-reliance and a contempt for dependency and weakness; superficial interpersonal and family ties and a striving for upward mobility through competition, achievement, and consumption.

Riesman et al. (1950) have described twentieth-century American character as "other-directed." The other-directed person is primarily an American product of the post-expansionist period. He is the archetypal "organization man," status-seeking, anxious for approval, and uncertain of his values (1950:40–41):

> the other-directed person learns to respond to signals from a far wider circle than is constituted by his parents. The family is no longer a closely knit unit to which he belongs but merely part of a wider social environment to which he early becomes attentive ... While the inner-directed person could be "at home abroad" by virtue of his relative insensitivity to others, the other-directed person is, in a sense, at home everywhere and nowhere, capable of a rapid if sometimes superficial intimacy with and response to everyone.

Riesman compares the other-directed type to previous types (tradition- and inner-directed) (1950:41–42):

> The tradition-directed person takes his signals from others, but they come in a cultural monotone; he needs no complex receiving equipment to pick them up. The other-directed person must be able to receive signals from far and near; the sources are many, the changes rapid. What can be internalized, then, is not a code of behavior but the equipment needed to attend to such messages and occasionally to participate in their circulation. As against guilt-and-shame controls, though of course these survive, one prime psychological lever of the other-directed person is a diffuse *anxiety*. This control equipment, instead of being like a gyroscope, is like a radar.

Although authors may disagree as to which of the preceding models best explains American character (e.g., Hsu 1972:245), there does not seem to be any major contradiction between Riesman's characterization and the other portraits. All of these authors agree that, compared to traditional societies, modern Americans have less stable identities and thus compete, consume, affiliate with status-conferring groups and individuals, and conform to changing fads in their search for identity and security. Although Riesman contends that other-directedness is largely a twentieth-century phenomenon, there is some evidence that Americans have always appeared other-directed to outsiders.

The French nobleman, Alexis de Tocqueville, visited America in 1831. From his stay of somewhat less than a year, he wrote his classic *Democracy in America*. In this work Tocqueville noted many of the same traits as the authors mentioned above: slavish conformity to public opinion, gross materialism, rampant competition, and a continual struggle for upward mobility. Tocqueville admired the self-reliance Americans showed when seeking personal fortune, but he also pointed out the disadvantages of this self-reliance (Tocqueville 1901, vol. 2: 786):

> As in ages of equality no man is compelled to lend assistance to his fellow-men, and none has any right to expect much support from them, every one is at once independent and powerless ... His independence fills him with self-reliance and pride among his equals; his debility makes him feel from time to time his want of some outward assistance, which he cannot expect from any of them, because they are all impotent and unsympathizing.

Lipset (1961) forcefully argues that, for almost two centuries, European visitors have consistently noted 'other-directed' qualities in Americans—qualities that Riesman ascribes to recent economic and demographic developments. Europeans have seen the American as shallower, more uncertain of himself and his values, and more approval-seeking than his European counterpart. In comparison, Europeans have always appeared (to themselves and to Americans) more tradition-directed—more bound by the traditional roles and rules of caste, church, and family. As an example, Lipset (1961:149) cites an American medical paper published in 1836; its resemblance to the sketches given above is striking:

> The population of the United States is beyond that of other countries an anxious one. All classes are either striving after wealth, or *endeavoring to keep up its appearance*. From the principle of imitation which is implanted in all of us, sharpened perhaps by the existing equality of conditions, the poor follow as closely as they are able the habits and manner of living of the rich ... From these causes, and perhaps from the nature of our political institutions, and the effects arising from them, we are an anxious, care-worn people.

In a recent discussion of American values (1975), Arensberg and Niehoff emphasize these same themes.

They point out that the American emphasis on self-reliance and achievement is essentially optimistic. That is, since everyone supposedly has equal opportunity, individuals are free to achieve as much success as their talent and effort warrant. These authors note, however, that the implications of this belief are not so optimistic: if it is assumed that all people can "make it" if they try, then those who do not make it are "failures" and should be despised and rejected (Arensberg and Niehoff 1975:371):

> This national confidence in effort and activity, with an optimism that trying to do something about a problem will almost invariably bring success in solving it, seems to be specifically American ... Serious effort to achieve success is both a personal goal and an ethical imperative. The worthwhile man is the one who "gets results" and "gets ahead" ... A failure in life "didn't have the guts" to "make a go of it" and "put himself ahead" ... [This code] raises serious problems. One of the most important is that it calls all those in high positions successes and all those in low ones "failures" even though everyone knows the majority must be in lower positions. A code of this sort by its very nature creates much frustration in all those who have not been able to achieve high positions.

Most authors agree that two factors were paramount in shaping these American traits (Tocqueville 1901; Henry 1963; Arensberg and Niehoff 1975). First, the open frontier, expanding economy, and virtually unlimited resources gave Americans the impression of limitless opportunity. Second, equality of opportunity was established as an ideal. In their official documents the founding fathers renounced the power of traditional institutions to ascribe status: all people were supposedly born equal and had equal rights before the law. Theoretically, then, people's social class, religion, and family ties should neither aid nor hinder their search for personal fortune. Given these assumptions, success through personal achievement became not only possible; it became mandatory. If certain individuals did not "get ahead," it was their own fault; they must be lazy or morally degenerate.

Implicit in the notion that a person must make something of himself is the assumption that behavior is not biologically predetermined. An individual's behavior can be worked on and developed; it does not inexorably unfold. In the absence of such predetermination, Americans apparently believe that environmental conditions (both social and material) are important determinants of behavior. Individuals, of course, are expected to exert personal effort in an attempt to arrange favorable environmental conditions. Mead (1968), for example, points out that "successful" American parents must provide their children with the proper environments. If parents want their children to succeed, they must provide them with a "good education" and "all the advantages they themselves didn't have."

The American themes of self-reliance, personal effort, and environmental causes thus seem to be complementary components in American conceptions. Because a person's behavior is not predetermined, he is both free and obligated to make something of himself. He must therefore exert an effort to improve himself. In doing so, he utilizes the environment, both physical and social, in striving to become a success. Similarly, he tries to provide the proper environmental input for his children, so that they may also "get ahead."

These themes of self-reliance, personal effort, and environmental influences appear to be reflected also in American conceptions of mental health (see Tables 1 and 3). Items 11, 32, 43, and 44 claim that immediate environmental conditions, like geographic location, financial status, job stress, and diet, can help determine a person's mental health. Items 45 and 55 also refer to environmental determinants: a person can *learn* to be mentally healthy. Similarly, items 35 and 40 stress the importance of the early years in shaping personality and mental health. Finally, the American themes of personal effort, optimism, and willpower are echoed in items 21, 27, and 42: to be mentally healthy, a person must discipline himself, avoid morbid thoughts, and keep busy. The American staff and student groups endorsed these items significantly more strongly than their German counterparts. American conceptions of mental illness thus seem to reflect more general cultural conceptions and value orientations.

Results: Factor 3

Factor 3: Negative Stereotypes

Factor 3, negative stereotypes, contained more specific conceptions of mental disorders than factor 1. Items comprised in this factor portrayed the mentally ill as recognizably different from "normal people." The mentally ill do not pay attention to personal appearance; they have glassy eyes, are incurable, and laugh more than normal people. Table 4 presents the items comprised in factor 3 and their loadings. The mean factor scores for the American and German student groups were −.025 and .162, respectively ($F = 15.10, df = 1/1278, P < .0001$). The American and German staff groups tended to reject this factor more strongly, with mean factor scores of −.457 and −.345, respectively. Although there was no significant difference between the two staff groups, they did differ significantly from their student groups in both countries ($P < .0001$). Table 5 presents the results of the four paired comparisons, which indicate that for this factor intracultural differences exceeded intercultural differences.

TABLE 4   Responses of German and American Staff and Students to Questionnaire Items Regarding Negative Stereotypes of the Mentally Ill (Factor 3)

Item	Loading	Means				Standard Deviations
		AStu	GStu	AS	GS	
14. The insane laugh more than normal people.	.51	2.8	3.2	2.3	1.9	1.72
37. You can tell a person who is mentally ill from his appearance.	.50	2.7	3.1	2.8	2.5	1.82
46. The eyes of the insane are glassy.	.46	2.9	2.8	1.9	1.8	1.62
22. There is not much that can be done for a person who develops a mental disorder.	.46	2.0	1.9	1.6	2.0	1.40

AStu = American high-school students ($N = 728$). GStu = German high-school students ($N = 555$). AS = American mental-hospital staff ($N = 79$). GS = German mental-hospital staff ($N = 102$). A mean of 7 signifies total agreement; a mean of 1, total disagreement; a mean of 4, neutrality. See text for description of samples and instrument.

TABLE 5   Analysis of Variance of Factor 3 Scores for German
and American Staff and Student Groups

	F	df	P <
Intracultural comparisons:			
American staff ($\bar{X} = -.46$) and students ($\bar{X} = -.025$)	18.83	1/805	.0001
German staff ($\bar{X} = -.35$) and students ($\bar{X} = .16$)	31.16	1/652	.0001
Intercultural comparisons:			
American and German staffs	0.92	1/179	—
American and German students	15.10	1/1278	.0005

American staff ($N = 79$); American students ($N = 728$); German staff ($N = 102$); German students ($N = 552$). See Appendix and text for description of samples and instruments.

Discussion: Factor 3

Factor 3 (negative stereotypes) distinguished between staff and public groups and between the student groups but it did not significantly differentiate the two staff groups, who tended to reject this factor more strongly than their publics. Factor 3, then, did not support hypothesis 1. This finding is probably partially explicable in terms of professional socialization. Hypothesis 2 posits that the common professional experiences of the two staff groups will tend to diminish differences between them. By the same token, this same shared experience could cause the staff groups to differ from the student groups in their responses to certain items. This may explain the groups' responses to factor 3. Factor 3 contains extremely negative stereotyped statements about the mentally ill: the insane laugh more than normal people, have glassy eyes, speak unintelligibly, and pay little attention to personal appearance. These are images that many mental-health specialists decry as derogatory stereotypes held by an ignorant public. The staff in a mental hospital know as a fact of experience that most mental patients do not laugh more than nonpatients (indeed, except for manic patients, they may laugh less); the staff also know that most patients do not have "glassy eyes," nor do they speak in unintelligible words. It is thus probably due to their actual experience (as well as to their desire to appear enlightened) that the hospital-staff groups in both countries tended to reject this factor as compared to the student groups. Thus, although these findings do not support hypothesis 1, they do tend to support hypothesis 2: professional socialization tends to diminish intercultural differences. The implications of these results for Scheff's theory will be discussed in chapter 2.

2 Patients' Conceptions of Mental Illness in Germany and America

The purpose of this chapter is to test propositions 2 and 3. Proposition 2 posited that the conceptions of mental disorders held by mental patients in Germany and America would show differences that corresponded to the differences in the two cultures' popular conceptions. Proposition 3 postulated that differences in symptom formation in the two cultures would correspond to differences in popular conceptions. In this investigation, symptoms per se were not studied, but interviews with patients did elicit statements about symptomatic behavior and coping tactics within the hospital. These statements will be analyzed and compared to the conceptions of mental illness in the two cultures.

Purpose

The following hypotheses were proposed:

Hypothesis 3. German and American mental patients have definite conceptions of mental illness. These conceptions parallel the conceptions held by mental-hospital staff and the public in their own cultures. Specifically, German patients, compared to American patients, view mental disorders as biological diseases that are relatively incurable. Americans, compared to Germans, emphasize environmental factors and personal effort in their conceptions of mental illness.

Parts of this chapter have appeared in my article "Cultural Conceptions and Mental Illness" in the *Journal of Nervous and Mental Disease* 160 (July, 1975): 409–21. Copyright © 1975 by The Williams & Wilkins Co. Reproduced by permission. Other parts appeared in my article "Cultural Conceptions, Mental Disorders, and Social Roles" in the *American Sociological Review* 40 (December, 1975): 739–52. Copyright © 1975 by the American Sociological Association. Reprinted by permission.

Hypothesis 4. Patients' perceptions of coping tactics reflect their conceptions of mental illness. Specifically, American patients endorse more strongly than German patients the view that a patient's release from the hospital depends on his personal effort: the patient must conform and make a good adjustment. German patients focus more on illness: the patient must be "cured" before he can be released.

Methods

Sample

Eighty-two German mental patients were selected and interviewed in a state mental hospital near Frankfurt, Germany. The patients were chosen randomly from the patient population except for strictly organic cases (e.g., cerebral arteriosclerosis, paresis), which were excluded.[1] A comparable sample of 98 patients was interviewed in a California state mental hospital. The hospitals were matched on important characteristics. Both are located in picturesque rural surroundings and are known as relatively pleasant places compared to other mental hospitals. Both draw the bulk of their patient populations from large urban centers, and most of their patients are usually admitted only after they have been processed and referred by other institutions. The demographic characteristics of the two patient populations are depicted in Table D in the Appendix.[2]

Instruments

In order to test the two hypotheses, a patient-interview schedule was constructed. Each patient interview lasted approximately three hours and often had to be completed on a second day. The coding categories used for each question during the interview were derived in a pilot study of 25 German patients. These categories were then used to analyze all subsequent patient interviews conducted in both Germany and America. In both cultures, assistants who were naive as to the specific hypotheses being tested did the bulk of the interviewing and coding. After the coders had been trained, periodic checks were made on inter-coder reliability. The reliability ranged from 85 to 95 percent.

The patient interview was designed to explore several areas of patient experience. These areas are as follows: (1)

conceptions of mental illness; (2) patients' perceptions of coping tactics; (3) patients' self-conceptions.

Part 1 of the interview was designed to reveal the patient's evaluation of himself and his situation—why he thought he was in the hospital and what he must do to get out. It consisted of twenty-four open-ended questions and a Twenty Statements Test (TST). The Twenty Statements Test requires that the subject complete the sentence "I am ..." twenty times. It has been used extensively in research on the self-concept of both patient and nonpatient groups. The coding categories, like the rest of the patient interview, were derived from the initial pilot study of German patients. It was found, however, that the responses did tend to fall into the broad categories suggested by Kuhn and McPartland (1954), and these categories were used, with minor modifications made wherever necessary. The categories were as follows:

1. *Physical*. This category includes all references to the subject's physical state, including his physical appearance (e.g., "I have blue eyes"; "I'm a man").

2. *State of health*. This category contained all references to the subject's state of health. This broad category was divided into three categories. Subcategory 1 included all references that were nonspecific ("I'm healthy"; "I'm sick"; "I'm a patient"). Subcategory 2 contained references to the subject's status and role as a mental patient ("I'm a mental patient") or direct allusions to life in the hospital ("I'm working in the canteen now"). Subcategory 3 encompassed statements which described the patient's official status ("I'm mentally ill"; "I'm schizophrenic"; "I have a nervous disorder"; "I'm an epileptic").

3. *Status and role in social system*. This category contained allusions to specific institutionally defined roles ("father," "lawyer," "Catholic," "married," "American," "Mason").

4. *Nature of interaction in the social system*. While category 3 contained allusions to institutional roles, e.g., "I'm a father," this category included all evaluation of such roles, e.g., "I'm a *good* father." It also contained references to activities that are not strictly defined institutional roles but do involve social interaction (e.g., "I'm a heavy drinker"; "I'm a baseball fan"; "I'm jolly").

5. *Inappropriate and uncodable answers.* This category consisted of responses that were uncodable either because they were inappropriate (e.g., "The cat is brown") or because they did not fit into any of the other categories (e.g., "I'm an iridescent being").

The results of part 1 of the patient-interview schedule were tested for significance with chi-square, except where the number of subjects in each category was too small to permit such analysis. For these questions, group differences are described in terms of percentages.[3]

Part 2 of the patient schedule consisted of five semantic differentials. The adjectival scales were adopted from Jaeckel and Wieser's study (1970) of German conceptions of mental illness. The concepts tested were: *Me, Psychiatrist, Patient in a Mental Hospital, Insane Person,* and *Average Person.* Jaeckel and Wieser had originally adopted many of Nunnally's adjectival scales (1961), so the problem of translating this instrument back into English was minimized. Nevertheless, a bilingual anthropologist was consulted in preparing the final English version.

Results: Conceptions

In order to compare the findings of this chapter more effectively with those of chapter 2, a distinction will be made between conceptions and stereotypes. The term conception refers to any opinion or belief about mental disorders, while *stereotype* refers specifically to negative views of mental illness like those embodied in factor 3 in chapter 1. These images portray the mentally ill as extremely bizarre, deviant, and disruptive. Conceptions will be discussed prior to stereotypes.

Conceptions of Mental Illness

Curability. Two questions tested curability. The first asked: "Is mental illness curable or not?" The response categories were: (1) No; (2) Cure no, improvement yes; (3) Many illnesses, yes; (4) All curable; (5) Yes, with enough therapeutic measures. A majority of Germans responded with answers 1–3, a majority of Americans with answers 4 and 5 ($P < .001$). The second question was similar in content. It asked: "What are the chances of curing someone who is mentally ill?'' Answer categories were: (1) Not curable; (2) 1 in 100; (3) 1 in 20; (4) 1 in 4; (5) 50:50; (6) All curable. The majority of Germans chose categories 1–4; the majority of Americans, 4–6 ($P < .01$). Thus, on both questions the German patients considered mental illness relatively incurable. These results tended to support hypothesis 1: German patients believe that mental illness is relatively incurable.

Purpose of Confinement. Germans and Americans differed markedly in their response to the question "Why are the mentally ill admitted to the hospital?" Although the number of responses in some categories was too small to permit statistical analysis, the percentages of responses for each group show striking differences. For example, 46 percent of German patients mentioned "improvement of health" as the reason that patients were committed; only 24 percent of the American group gave this response. In contrast, only 2 percent of German patients stated "because they behaved in a 'crazy' [in the stereotyped sense] manner," while over 12 percent of the Americans cited this as the reason for commitment. The results on curability and confinement indicate that the conceptions of mental illness differ markedly in the two countries. Compared to American patients, German patients believe that mental illness is a biological disease that is relatively incurable and that does not necessarily manifest itself in bizarre behavior.

Patient Perceptions of Coping Tactics. Patients were asked who influenced their release and how it could be obtained. The results are presented in Table 6. Americans in general tended to believe that a patient's release depends on his personal effort: the patient must conform and make a good adjustment within the hospital. In contrast, German patients focused more on illness: the doctor must decide that the patient is well. These results tended to support proposition 2, that patients' conceptions of mental illness parallel those of their staff and public. Hypotheses 3 and 4 were also supported. The patient groups' perceptions of coping tactics echoed the basic cultural themes reviewed in chapter 1. In the American patients' view, a patient's release depended on his personal effort and willpower, on his ability to manipulate himself and his environment. For the Germans, there was nothing a patient could "do" to expedite his release. The doctor would know when he was "well" and would discharge him. Thus, patients' statements on curability, reasons for confinement, and coping tactics all reflected the same cultural differences examined

TABLE 6   German and American Patients' Perceptions of Appropriate Coping Tactics within Hospital

Questions	Percentage of German Patients	Percentage of American Patients
1. "In your opinion who influences your release?"		
a. "Myself."	1.2	20.4
b. "The doctors" (or doctors in combination with other factors).	79.3	49.0
2. "How does [*patient's answer to above question*] decide that someone should be released?"		
a. "Patient must conform, play the game, obey the rules ... "	8.5	27.6
b. "[*Answer from 'b' in above question*] decides when the patient is well."	42.7	17.3
3. "How must a patient behave in order to be released?"		
a. (Patient gives one or more examples of adjusted behavior.)	4.9	46.9
b. "Patient must be well."	12.2	5.1
c. "Patient must be well and adjusted" (one or more examples)	36.6	5.1
d. (A number of examples of adjusted behavior, with or without recovery).	36.6	26.5
4. "What should the patient never do if he wants to be released?"		
a. "Never misbehave" (one or more examples).	2.4	52.0
b. "Patient must not be 'ill.' "	13.4	1.0
c. "Patient must not be 'ill' " (with one or more examples of maladaptive behavior).	34.1	0.0
d. (More than one example of maladaptive behavior, with or without recovery.)		

German patients ($N = 82$); American patients ($N = 98$).

in chapter 1: Germans view mental illness as relatively determinate; Americans emphasize free will, personal effort, and manipulating one's self and the environment.

Twenty Statements Test. As noted above, the patient groups also completed a Twenty Statements Test. This test requires that the respondent complete the sentence "I am ... " twenty times. The answers were coded (see the section on Methods, above) and subjected to chi-square tests. The results generally tended to support hypothesis 3. Compared to the American patients, the German patients tended to "somaticize" their condition. They talked of physical ailments and generally emphasized the *medical* nature of their hospitalization ($P < .001$). In contrast, American patients made more allusions to roles performed *within* the hospital. They talked more about their behavior as mental patients ($P < .01$). These findings are consistent with hypothesis 3 and with the preceding results. In their self-conceptions, as well as in their conceptions of mental disorders and coping tactics, the Germans tended to emphasize biomedical factors. They tended to see the hospital as a hospital, the doctors as physicians, and the reasons for confinement as medical.

Discussion: Conceptions

The German sample contained a greater percentage of patients over forty years of age. To test for possible effects of this bias, the two samples were divided into two age groups: under forty and over forty. These groups were then compared, using chi-square, on each of the questions discussed above. Only one question showed a significant difference between age groups ($P < .06$). In answer to the question "When can you say someone is crazy?" younger American patients tended to have "no opinion," while their older counterparts tended to reject the question due to its pejorative connotations. This difference cannot explain the difference on this question between Germans and Americans because that difference arose from more Germans citing mental characteristics, while more Americans named physical (stereotyped) characteristics.

The American sample was biased toward voluntary

commitments. The two patient samples were therefore divided into groups on the basis of type of commitment: voluntary or involuntary. Only the German groups differed significantly, and then on only two questions. More voluntary German patients gave more pessimistic answers to the question "Is mental illness curable or not?" This difference cannot explain the difference found between the German and American samples because more Germans tended to give pessimistic answers than Americans and the German sample was biased toward *involuntary* commitments. The last question of the interview was more problematic. In answer to the question "Why are the mentally ill admitted to the hospital?" more involuntary German patients cited reasons of health ($P < .03$). More Germans than Americans cited such reasons, so the sample bias might explain this difference between the two cultural groups. I believe this is unlikely, for the following reasons. First, the German sample took a similar "medical" stance on several other measures in the interview (e.g., questions on curability, coping tactics, and the Twenty Statements Test). These questions showed no significant differences between types of confinement. Second, most of the American "voluntary" patients had previously been involuntary but had eventually been "persuaded" to commit themselves. Voluntary commitments were more convenient for the California hospital staff because of laws protecting patients' rights, which had recently been passed (Lanterman-Petris-Short Act, 1969). According to ethnographic observations, involuntary commitments did not at that time in Germany present much more of a problem than voluntary ones (e.g., in respect to more paper work, more frequent reviews, court appearances). Consequently, the staff did not pressure patients to commit themselves. I thus think that the discrepancy in percentages of voluntary commitments in the two samples does not reflect substantive social or psychological differences between the samples but rather the utility and plasticity of labels for regulating patient populations. Third, there were fewer than twenty voluntary commitments in the German sample. This made for very few responses in each of the answer categories for each question. Such small cell sizes could create artifacts. Finally, in the American sample, type of confinement showed *no* significant differences on any of the questions. It therefore appears that the effects of the age and type of commitment bias in the two samples cannot account for the differences found between the two cultural groups.

The results of this section thus tended to support proposition 2 and hypotheses 3 and 4. Mental patients' conceptions in Germany and America corresponded to the differences in the two cultures' popular conceptions of mental illness. Relative to Americans, German patients tended to emphasize the biomedical, determinate nature of mental illness. In contrast, Americans stressed personal effort and environmental factors in their conceptions. The present research thus suggests that cultural conceptions, or beliefs about mental illness, do help to shape certain patient behaviors (at least their interview responses and their statements about proper behavior within the hospital). The evidence for this proposition comes from two sources. First, the German patients' conceptions of mental illness differed significantly from those of the American patients. German patients generally agreed with their staff and public that mental illness is an endogenous biological malady that is virtually incurable. In contrast, the American groups tended to see mental illness more as a behavioral phenomenon. For the Americans, "mental illness" resided in behavioral deviance rather than in an innate organic condition. In the American view, this deviance can be eliminated with the right combination of motivation, skill, and willpower on the part of the patient and physician.

The two groups' self-conceptions also differed significantly. German patients tended to somaticize their conditions and reasons for confinement. Americans talked about their roles as mental patients. These same themes were reflected in the reasons patients gave for confinement in a mental hospital. Germans tended to mention "improvement of health" as the reason patients are committed to a mental hospital. Americans more frequently cited "crazy" behavior as the reason for commitment. These results thus tended to confirm hypothesis 3.

Second, the groups' conceptions of mental illness were

consistent with their perceptions of appropriate coping tactics within the hospital. For the German patients, only the doctor could decide when a patient should be released; there was nothing the patient could do to influence this medical decision. In contrast, the Americans emphasized behavior and voluntary acts as crucial to the patient's discharge. In this regard they stressed compliance with hospital regulations and staff directives. Thus, as in the case of hypothesis 3, the Germans tended to assume a sort of biological-deterministic position, while the Americans maintained more of an individual-responsibility–free-will stance. These results tended to support hypothesis 4.

As was argued in chapter 1, this assumption of "behavioral free will" is perhaps one of the most consistent themes in American ideology, and it has been noted by numerous observers over the past two centuries. Relative to most other peoples, Americans assume that an individual is free to alter his behavior and make anything of himself he desires. Thus, if a person is poor or mentally ill, it is somehow his own fault. "He could have made it if he had really tried!" Some of the broader implications of this American value orientation will be discussed in subsequent chapters.

Results: Negative Stereotypes
Patient Self-Conceptions

Interview questions.   A variety of measures were used to study patients' self-conceptions and their conceptions of other patients. These measures gave the respondent an opportunity to use stereotyped imagery in reference to himself or other patients if he was so inclined. The first measure consisted of a series of open-ended questions within the patient interview. For example, question 3 asked: "Do you believe that you belong in the mental hospital? Why, or why not?" This question revealed no significant cultural differences. Approximately 35 percent of both the American and the German patient groups stated that they thought they belonged in the hospital. Approximately 50 percent of each group believed that they did not belong. The remainder were "uncertain." Question 17 asked: "Do you consider yourself mentally ill? Why, or why not?" Approximately 25 percent of the American group answered "Yes," while only 9 percent of the German group answered in the affirmative ($P < .01$). The rest of the samples answered "No."

Question 12 asked: "Do the other patients belong in the hospital? Why, or why not?" Question 16 asked: "Are the other patients mentally ill? Why, or why not?" Only 7 percent of the German patients said that they did not belong in the hospital but that the others did. Seventeen percent of the Americans gave this answer ($P < .05$). Similarly, 4 percent of the Germans and 25 percent of the Americans claimed that the other patients were ill but that they themselves were not ($P < .001$). Thus, in these comparisons, more Germans identified with patients they did not view as mentally ill. More Americans tended to lump the other patients into the "sick" category and to reject identification with them. Neither patient group, however, tended to define themselves as mentally ill, although more Americans (25 percent) did than Germans (9 percent). Virtually no stereotyped imagery appeared in these responses.

Twenty Statements Test. This instrument also gave the patients an opportunity to use stereotyped imagery in their self-descriptions. The two cultural groups did not differ in their tendency to describe themselves in terms of stereotypes or diagnostic labels. In fact, the overwhelming majority of both groups did not use any such terms in their self-descriptions: only four Americans and eight Germans referred to themselves with diagnostic labels.

Semantic differentials. The final instruments used to measure patients' self-conceptions were the semantic differentials. The results of these instruments were first analyzed in an overall analysis of variance (2 x 5 x 6 factorial) on the five general concepts *Me, Pyschiatrist, Patient in a Mental Hospital, Insane Person,* and *Average Person.* For this analysis, semantic dimensions that have consistently emerged in cross-cultural research were assumed, and the respective adjectival scales were grouped into these semantic dimensions (Osgood 1969; Nunnally 1961; Jaeckel and

Wieser 1970). The six dimensions used were evaluation, potency, activity, certainty, understandability, and predictability. In this overall analysis, the two patient groups did not differ significantly; consequently, no further comparisons were made of these groups. The German staff and student samples described in chapter 1 also completed the semantic differentials. The patient groups rated the concept *Me* significantly more *positively* than did the German staff and student groups ($P < .01$). Though significant, the differences were slight: patient means ranged from 2.3 to 2.7; staff and public means, from 2.7 to 3.1 (the higher the mean, the more negative the evaluation). Thus, once again, patients avoided using negative stereotyped imagery in describing themselves.

Stereotypes of Insanity

Americans differed significantly from Germans ($P < .001$) in response to the question "How can you recognize a mentally ill person?" More Americans cited stereotyped bizarre physical characteristics as "diagnostic" criteria. In contrast, the German patients more frequently favored "internal" criteria, i.e., they tended to cite disturbances of mental functions, cognition, and judgment as characterizing mental illness. This difference, although highly significant, reflects a tendency rather than an absolute difference: only 27 percent of the American group picked physical characteristics ("the way he looks"; "from his face"; "from his eyes"; "walks funny"); only 13 percent of the German sample cited these characteristics. In contrast, 20 percent of the German patients picked disturbances of mental functions, while only 2 percent of the Americans fell within this category. This category contained only those answers that were reasonable approximations of official psychiatric theory. Thus, more Germans consistently assumed a medical view of things.

Discussion: Negative Stereotypes

As reported above, mental patients' conceptions in Germany and America generally paralleled the conceptions held by professionals and students in their own country. These results tended to support hypotheses 1 and 2. In contrast, the patients, like their staff and public groups in chapter 1, tended to avoid using stereotypes. In response to the question "How can you recognize a mentally ill person?" only a minority of patients in either group mentioned stereotyped images of insanity. Similarly, in answer to the question "Why are the mentally ill admitted to the hospital?" less than a third of the patients cited negative stereotypes of insanity. Finally, a majority of patients in both groups denied that they themselves were mentally ill, and a majoirty failed to identify with patients they thought were mentally ill. In short, a majority of patients declined to use stereotyped images of insanity, and a majority of patients denied they were mentally ill and failed to identify with patients they thought were mentally ill.

The patients' relative rejection of the stereotypes of insanity and their disinclination to use these images in descriptions of themselves and others are thus consistent with the staff and student groups' responses to factor 3. None of the groups strongly endorsed this factor. Apparently, the results of factors 1–3 and the patient data are consistent with a general application of labeling theory to mental disorders: general cultural conceptions appear to influence patient behavior (at least, the conceptions appear to influence patient conceptions and perceptions of proper behavior). In contrast, the results of factor 3 and the patient data do *not* support Scheff's application (1966) of labeling theory to mental disorders: stereotypes of insanity (of the type discussed by Scheff) did not appear frequently in patients' conceptions or in their perceptions of proper coping behavior. To interpret this finding, it is useful to recapitulate the logic of this investigation and to examine some background material bearing on Scheff's theory and the present results.

Conceptions versus Stereotypes

Walter Lippmann was the first to introduce and delineate the concept of *stereotype* (1930). He argued that stereotypes arise from the fact that all perception is selective. The brain cannot possibly perceive and evaluate all the sensations impinging on it, so it selects out what is important. For example, a mother, working in the house, may not perceive the sound of the cars passing outside, but she will hear her child's cry—even though the cars may objectively be louder. This selective process is largely automatic and is a product of an individual's cultural conditioning. Cultural training, then, not only selects what we perceive, but it also determines how we feel about it.

The myriad stimuli impinging upon an individual's sensory apparatus are sorted into classes, or categories, and these categories are, to some extent, culturally conditioned. A person from another culture will group and evaluate stimuli differently. As Lippmann points out (1930:90), this grouping affords an economy of perception and is apparently a necessary part of perception. But because the grouping is largely automatic, it is subject to unconscious distortion and prejudice.

It is this grouping and evaluation process that can obscure important differences among members of a group and ultimately result in maleficent prejudice. As Lippmann points out, stereotypes are constantly used to justify our actions and our position in society. To justify slavery, slaves must be perceived as intrinsically different from other men; to justify war, the enemy must be portrayed as incorrigibly evil; and to justify racial oppression, the other race must be seen as something less than human. Stereotypes thus prevent us from objectively evaluating facts, and, although they are inevitable, we need to recognize them, to "hold them lightly, and modify them gladly" (Lippmann, 1930:91)

Klapp (1972) criticizes Lippmann as being "rationalistic" and argues that the term stereotype implies distortion and prejudice. He therefore prefers "social type" as a conceptual tool in his analysis of American slang terms that denote certain types of character (e.b., "good Joe," "party-pooper," "do-gooder"). Klapp maintains that social types are quite accurate and that they perform the following useful functions for society: (1) they allow people to recognize and play various roles; (2) they help define emergent roles; (3) they aid professionalization, i.e., help fit the right man to the right job; (4) they provide a person with self-images and a way of fitting into the larger system; (5) they aid in status modification (e.g., degradation); (6) they contribute to consensus. In sum, Klapp feels that social typing helps society set normative limits and orient its members. Because typing does this, and because it is inevitable, the effects of typing should be viewed as benign. Whether these effects are benign or not is, of course, a value judgment. [4] Keeping this in mind, we can utilize some parts of Klapp's analysis. His discussion of the effects of social types is quite cogent; it is whether these effects are beneficial or not that is questionable.

The fourth function Klapp proposes for social types is that they provide a person with self-images and a way of relating to the social system. These images may be positive and admirable (Heroes), or they may be negative and repellent (Villains and Fools). Thus, when a person is typed (e.g., as a do-gooder), the image provides guidelines for his behavior and for those around him. If people see him that way, they will encourage him (sometimes inadvertently) to act that way. An individual may thus orient his behavior according to an acceptable social type, or he may use negative images to portray what is unacceptable behavior. This latter use is essentially the function of *contrast conception*.

In his discussion of the stereotypes of mental illness, Scheff (1966:78) argues that the stereotypes of ethnic groups or of the mentally ill serve as "reference points for social comparisons and self-evaluation." That is, they serve as contrast conceptions. Scheff proceeds in this part of his analysis to stress the *distorted* nature of stereotypes. That is to say, the stereotypes of mental illness may have *some* basis in reality, but they are not representative of reality, since only a minority of cases actually correspond to the stereotypes. Scheff illustrates this point when he compares stereotypes of the mentally ill to racial stereotypes, when he reveals the biased reporting in newspaper accounts of mental illness, and when he compares the popular stereotypes of the insane as "violent" and "dangerous" with a statistical study that showed that former mental patients actually committed fewer violent crimes than the general population (1966:67–79). Thus, in this part of Scheff's discussion, the stereotypes of mental illness represent the most extreme and bizarre forms of the phenomenon, and they consequently tend to exaggerate the differences between "normal" and insane behavior. In this sense, Scheff presents the stereotypes as a distortion of reality.

On the other hand, Scheff tells us that the stereotypes act as a guide for action, shaping amorphous rule-breaking in their own image (1966:82). Through this process, the roles of mental illness will increasingly resemble the stereotypes. This is essentially Klapp's "function 1": social types allow people to recognize and play various roles. According to this part of Scheff's theory, then, *some* mental illness must ultimately resemble the stereotypes, but we are never told what kind or how much. Consequently, we never know in what sense the stereotypes are "stereotypes," i.e., how they deviate from reality. The problem of defining stereotypes is thus central to Scheff's theory. To define "stereotypes" rigorously, Scheff would have had to describe the degree of their correspondence to reality. In doing so, he would have automatically commented on the efficacy of the stereotypes as shapers of the roles of mental illness.

This problem, however, is not unique to Scheff's discussion of stereotypes. Brigham, for example, in his review (1971:31–32) of the literature on ethnic stereotypes, notes that criteria for judging the accuracy or distortion of stereotypes are typically lacking in such research:

> the major shortcoming of most of the published "stereotype" research ... has been a failure on the part of these observers to make explicit the criteria under which they are considering the generalizations unjustified. And, in those cases where criteria have been described, such as factual incorrectness, representations of inferior judgmental processes, or justifications for discriminatory behavior, it has usually been left unsaid that these criteria remain assumptions on the part of the particular researchers, rather than measurable attributes of the situation.

Compared to ethnic stereotypes, the problem of judging the accuracy of stereotypes of insanity may be simpler. With regard to two of the more common stereotypes, the evidence suggests that actual behavior does *not* conform to the stereotypes. Numerous authors have isolated an image of unpredictable violence as one of the essential components in the stereotypes of insanity (Nunnally 1961; Cumming and Cumming 1957; Jaeckel and Wieser 1970; Olmsted and Durham 1976). Contrary to the stereotypes, Scheff cites a statistical study which showed that the incidence of violent crime (or of any crime) is much lower among former mental patients than in the general population (1966:72).

Even more compelling are the results of the *Baxstrom* decision. In 1966 a United States Supreme Court decision forced institutions for the criminally insane to transfer many of their patients to civil hospitals. Steadman and Cocozza (1974) analyzed the results of this decision in New York State. Of 967 patients transferred to civil hospitals, about 25 percent were eventually discharged to the community. The transfer and discharge of *Baxstrom* patients aroused intense anxiety in civil hospitals and the community. These fears proved to be totally unjustified. A four-year follow-up study showed that only 2 of the 98 patients (in the study sample) released to the community were subsequently convicted of felonies (namely, armed robbery and grand larceny). This seems a modest percentage when one compares it to the recidivism rates for ex-convicts (or to the incidence of violence and crime in urban high schools). It seems especially modest when one considers that these patients were considered extremely dangerous and had for years consistently been denied transfer or discharge.

Another popular image of insanity is that of delusional personalities (Nunnally 1961; Scheff 1966:75). The mentally ill are frequently depicted in the mass media as having delusions of grandeur: these persons believe they are Christ, Napoleon, or some other famous personality. In his search for delusional personalities among 25,000 patients in state mental hospitals in Michigan, Rokeach (1964) found only a handful of such people; only three patients without brain damage consistently believed they were Christ, and there were no Napoleons, Caesars, Khrushchevs, or Eisenhowers. Thus, although stereotypes may influence symptoms, they do not seem to act as a "guideline for behavior," as Scheff has proposed.

Another problem with Scheff's theory is that he ignores the role of the hospital. His theory proposes that the *popu-*

lar stereotypes of insanity, culturally reinforced since childhood, act as a model in shaping the roles of insanity. These stereotypes supposedly act as a guideline for behavior for the deviant and for those around him, gradually forcing his behavior into ever-increasing conformity with the stereotypes. There is no direct evidence, however, that mental-hospital staff members have internalized stereotyped images of insanity which they then inadvertently reinforce in the behavior of patients. The most common stereotype, that of wild, uncontrollable, dangerous behavior, is certainly controlled and often directly punished by the staff. It is true that bizarre behaviors may be reinforced inadvertently by the staff (usually because that is the only way the patient receives staff attention), but these behaviors do not appear to be those contained in popular stereotypes (Levitz and Ullmann 1969; Fontana and Klein 1968; Braginsky et al. 1966). In fact, participant-observation studies tend to mention more passive behaviors: sitting and staring, aimlessly pacing, rocking, perhaps arguing with staff or other patients, and working for insignificant rewards (Goffman 1961; Rosenhan 1973, 1975; Goldman et al. 1973). Furthermore, the results of my study suggest that staff members in Germany and America endorse stereotypes *less* than their respective publics, so any serious attempt to validate Scheff's theory would have to make detailed comparisons between the conceptions of staff and public and the symptomatic behaviors *each* tends to reinforce. The role of the hospital in producing symptomatic behavior will be discussed more thoroughly in chapter 4.

A final flaw in the stereotype theory concerns the apparent lack of a coherent folk model of mental illness in urban populations. No empirical study has been able to demonstrate such a model. To be sure, Germany appears to have a somewhat more systematic folk taxonomy than America (Jaeckel and Wieser 1970; Nunnally 1961), but even in Germany the public's answers showed considerable variation and disagreement. Moreover, to warrant the term "model," folk conceptions of illness generally contain some notions of diagnostic criteria, etiology, prognoses, and treatment arranged in some reasonably coherent framework (e.g., Wallace 1972). No such models for mental disorders have been demonstrated in lay populations of industrialized nations. Compared to large nation-states, the societies where folk models have been described are consensual communities. In such communities, virtually everyone subscribes to the same supernatural beliefs, and theories of illness are generally an integral part of these beliefs. Such theories, then, have the force of powerful sanctions behind them, and, because there is virtual consensus on these theories, persons surrounding the deviant are probably more consistent in reinforcing or punishing various behaviors. It is probably due to this consensus and consistency that folk conceptions appear to be more effective in structuring illness behavior in small primitive societies than in large nation-states.

All this suggests that a clear distinction should be made between popular stereotypes and popular conceptions. The type of stereotypes discussed by Scheff are the extreme images of insanity popularly depicted in the mass media; they are essentially the images embodied in factor 3, which were not strongly endorsed by any of the groups I studied. It is thus quite possible that the stereotypes do not structure symptomatology in the manner Scheff proposed. On the other hand, cultural *conceptions* of mental disorders, as embodied in factor 1, did appear in patient conceptions and in their descriptions of proper coping tactics. This suggests that cultural conceptions, or beliefs about mental illness, do influence patient perceptions and coping tactics. It is therefore quite possible that these conceptions affect overt symptomatology as well.

If stereotypes of the extreme type discussed by Scheff do not effectively structure symptomatology in the manner he proposed, what role, if any, do they play in the societal reaction to deviance? In the following paragraphs, I would like to depart somewhat from my empirical findings and elaborate on Jaeckel and Wieser's analysis (1970) of the stereotypes of insanity. To be sure, the functions for stereotypes proposed below do not derive directly from the results presented in this chapter. Nevertheless, the proposed functions are entirely consistent with the present results and with other empirical studies to be discussed.

Functions of Stereotypes

One of the most consistent elements in society's reaction to mental illness is fear. This is reflected in empirical studies (Cumming and Cumming 1957; Nunnally 1961; Jaeckel and Wieser 1970) and in the laws society has erected to protect itself (Steadman and Cocozza 1974). Jaeckel and Wieser argue that, although the public fears physical threats from the insane, the real threat is to the background understandings and expectations that make social intercourse possible. Unlike other deviants, the mentally ill appear to the lay public to have incomprehensible motives and to be impervious to threats of punishment and other sanctions. They thus appear both unpredictable and uncontrollable. It is this fantasy of uncontrollability that provokes such intense fear.[6]

This scheme receives support from two sources. First, empirical studies have isolated "unpredictability" and "incomprehensibility" as consistent components in the images urban populations have of the mentally ill (Nunnally 1961; Townsend 1972; Jaeckel and Wieser 1970). Second, it appears that people in small communities, who are more familiar with a deviant individual, tend to find his behavior more comprehensible and predictable and are thus more likely to tolerate certain eccentricities (Foucault 1965; Eaton and Weil 1967); Scheff (1966), for example, found that rural courts were more careful about commitments and generally more tolerant of eccentric behavior than urban courts.

In line with the preceding argument, three functions for the stereotypes of insanity may be proposed. First, they may serve as a warning, a contrast conception, to those who would breach social expectations. Phrases like "That's crazy!" or "Better watch out—they'll be calling the men in the white coats!", though often used facetiously, nevertheless protest against unexpected rule violations; they tell a person his behavior is not quite acceptable. This function corresponds to Klapp's function 4, that is, social types (and contrast conceptions) provide a person with self-images and a way of fitting into the larger system.

Second, the stereotypes may function as diagnostic criteria for the layman. For the man in the street, stereotypes may provide a guide for detecting insane behavior. As pointed out above, however, the stereotypes are *not* accurate depictions of symptomatology. One would therefore expect the public's recognition threshold to be high; i.e., initial symptoms that did not match the stereotypes would not be perceived as mental illness. This appears to be the case. Yarrow et al. (1955) found that husbands had to breach their wives' expectations repeatedly before the wives would finally define the behavior as mental illness. Similarly, Star (1955) found that, when presented with classic textbook examples of various mental disorders, the public designated only the most extreme case, paranoid schizophrenia, as mental illness. Evidently, these studies tend to support the notion that the public's recognition threshold remains high partially because their images of mental illness are so distorted. Once the recognition threshold is crossed, however, the stereotypes serve to justify the extreme, dichotomous treatment of the mentally ill. This is a third possible function of the stereotypes. The distorted images of the stereotypes then justify total isolation of the deviant and the suspension of his rights and duties. This occurs even though a person's behavior may have indicated that less extreme measures were in order (because, in fact, his behavior did not conform to the stereotypes). Even when this is the case—as it usually is—the fear is always present that his behavior might conform to the stereotypes in the future. These functions would correspond to Klapp's functions 5 and 6: stereotypes aid in status modification, and they contribute to consensus.[7]

Although these functions for the stereotypes of insanity are not directly supported by the results of this study, they are nevertheless consistent with them and with other empirical works. Consistent with the present findings, then, is the notion that the stereotypes, though not frequently realized in symptomatology, may well serve as warnings, as folk diagnostic criteria, and as rationalizations for the extreme treatment of the mentally ill.

Conclusion

To sum up this chapter: broad cultural conceptions of

mental disorders differ in Germany and America, and the conceptions of patients, mental-hospital staff, and laymen within these countries parallel each other quite closely. Thus, intercultural differences exceeded intracultural differences. In contrast, cultural stereotypes of insanity were not consistently endorsed by patients, staff, or students in either country. Stereotypes were also lacking in patients' self-conceptions and their perceptions of proper behavior within the hospital. These findings thus provide some support for a general application of labeling theory to mental disorders: cultural conceptions do appear to influence patients' perceptions. The present results do not, however, support Scheff's specific application (1966) of labeling theory, i.e., that the stereotypes of insanity act as a guideline for symptom formation. The present findings thus establish a definite link between cultural conceptions of mental illness and patient views of appropriate coping tactics. It is not yet clear, however, how cultural conceptions may affect a wider range of patient behavior. The exact relationships among patient behavior, different conceptions of mental illness, and the formal requirements of institutional life have yet to be delineated. These problems will be discussed in more detail in chapter 3.

3   Institutionalization and Symptomatology

In the preceding chapter, the evidence examined did not support the theory that specific stereotypes of insanity mold specific symptoms of mental illness. The evidence did suggest, however, that mental patients in Germany and America shared certain conceptions of mental illness with their respective publics and professionals. Furthermore, these conceptions were reflected in the patient groups' statements about symptoms and coping behavior within the hospital. Thus, the evidence marshaled above does *not* indicate that the public and the mental-hospital staff are inadvertently but effectively reinforcing stereotyped symptoms in the patients' behavior. This raises the question of what role the hospital does play in symptom formation. The purpose of this chapter is to examine the effects of long-term hospitalization on symptoms and patient outcome.

Discussions of institutionalization have generally derived from two different approaches. The first approach can be termed, for want of a better word, the "conversion" approach and is exemplified by the works of Goffman (1961), Gruenberg (1967), and Zusman (1973). These authors—often more implicitly than explicitly—approach the phenomenon of institutionalization through the notion of basic changes in self-concept. They argue that the hospital "converts" the patient, i.e., that the patient eventually comes to accept the hospital's definition of him as sick.

Parts of this chapter have appeared in my article "Cultural Conceptions and Mental Illness" in the *Journal of Nervous and Mental Disease* 160 (July, 1975) 409–21. Copyright © 1975 by The Williams &Wilkins Co. Reproduced by permission. Other parts have appeared in my article "Self-Concept and the Institutionalization of Mental Patients" in the *Journal of Health and Social Behavior* 17 (September, 1976): 263–71. Copyright © 1976 by the American Sociological Association. Reprinted by permission.

When this conversion is complete, the patient fully believes he is sick, acts sick, and is thus incapable of operating effectively outside the hospital. The second approach is more behavioral. It tends to operationalize its concepts and focus more on observable behavior. Authors utilizing this approach do not postulate that the institutionalization of mental patients necessarily consists in the hospital's convincing the patient that he is sick. Instead, these authors tend to define a patient as institutionalized if he is apathetic about leaving the hospital. Some articles begin by paying homage to the conversion approach but then proceed to take a more behavioral approach in their methodology and discussions (Wing 1962; Shiloh 1971). In this chapter I will argue (1) that the changes in self-concept proposed by the conversion approach have yet to be demonstrated, (2) that the vagueness of the conversion approach has resulted in some questionable interpretations of the nature of the mental hospital, and (3) that, in empirical study, a more behavioral approach has obviated many of the problems created by the conversion approach.

For the purpose of this argument, the term "institutionalization" will refer to the effects an institution has on an inmate that progressively reduce his ability to live outside the institution. Stemming from the verb form "to institutionalize," the term institutionalization implies an emphasis on process rather than on a static phenomenon. Thus, institutionalization, as used here, refers to the process of inmates' becoming progressively incapable of living outside the institution because of the effects, planned or inadvertent, of the institution upon him.

The Conversion Approach

Probably the leading exponent of the conversion approach is Erving Goffman. In his now classic study, *Asylums* (1961), Goffman proposed that the mental hospital, in order to effect compliance with its institutional needs, brings the patient to accept its view of him as a mental patient (1961:155). To accomplish this often requires that the patient's view of himself be discredited. Goffman argues that psychotherapy and group therapy frequently perform this function (usually inadvertently) (1961:366–77).

Indeed, Goffman asserts that the more progressive and therapeutic the hospital attempts to be, the more it will tend to discredit the patient's self-definition, replacing it with its own definition of him as mentally ill (Goffman 1961:150). According to this logic, the more "progressive" hospitals might induce even more institutionalization than custodial institutions because the former are more likely to succeed in changing the patient's self-concept. This logic is exemplified in the following quotations:

> What we have here [in institutional therapy sessions] is a direct ... effort to transform the patient in his own eyes into a closed system in need of servicing (Goffman 1961:376–77).
>
> ... the more it [the hospital] attempts to be therapeutic and not merely custodial—the more he [the patient] may be confronted by high-ranking staff arguing that ... if he wants to be a person he will have to change his way of dealing with people and his conceptions of himself (Goffman 1961:150).
>
> He [the patient] learns that a defensible picture of self can be seen as something outside oneself that can be constructed, lost, and rebuilt, all with great speed and with some equanimity. He learns about the viability of taking up a standpoint—and hence a self—that is outside the one which the hospital can give and take away from him (Goffman 1961:165).
>
> The patient must "insightfully" come to take, or affect to take, the hospital's view of himself (Goffman 1961:155).

These quotations clearly suggest that the institutionalization of mental patients consists in converting them; i.e., the patients must come to accept the hospital's view of them as ill and "in need of servicing."

Zusman's theory of institutionalization is similar to Goffman's. Summarizing previous work by himself and Gruenberg (Gruenberg and Zusman 1964), Zusman (1973) describes institutionalization in terms of the "social-breakdown syndrome." This syndrome has seven basic stages: (1) precondition or susceptibility: deficiency in self-concept; (2) dependence on current cues; (3) social labeling as incompetent and dangerous; (4) induction into the sick role; (5) learning the chronic sick role; (6) atrophy of work and social skills; and (7) identification with the sick.

Zusman (1973:312) equates the last stage with Goffman's "conversion" and states that "At some point the chronic state of sick functioning is not only accepted by the patient but he comes to see himself as like the other sick people with whom he lives, and no longer looks on himself as exceptional." Zusman has thus extraverted and made explicit what was largely implicit in Goffman. Both authors point to role changes via changes in self-conception as the crucial dynamic in institutionalization. That is, mental patients come to believe they are mentally ill, and they act accordingly. As intuitively plausible as this theory is, there is little empirical evidence to support it.

The Empirical Evidence

Empirical studies of mental patients have consistently failed to demonstrate that mental patients think of themselves as mentally ill. The Joint Commission on Mental Illness and Health, for example, found that acutely ill patients in mental hospitals do not consider themselves mentally ill and in need of help (1961:86). Levinson and Gallagher (1964) reported that a majority of patients in their sample denied they were mentally ill. Similarly, Braginsky et al. (1969:64) found that 78 percent of a sample of 189 patients agreed with the questionnaire statement "Most patients in a state mental hospital are not mentally ill." Agreement with this item was uncorrelated with length of hospitalization. This led the authors to conclude that long-term patients were *not* more likely to view other patients (and themselves) as mentally ill.

The German and American patient groups I studied also failed to show the proposed changes in self-concept. It will be remembered that a majority of patients in both groups denied they were mentally ill. In response to the question "Do you consider yourself mentally ill?", 91 percent of the Germans and 75 percent of the Americans answered in the negative. A related question asked, "Do you belong in the hospital?" Approximately 50 percent of each group felt that they did *not* belong. Approximately 35 percent of each group felt they belonged. The rest were uncertain. Moreover, most patients in both groups did not believe that a majority of the other patients belonged in the hospital or

were mentally ill. The patients' answers to these questions
were not correlated with length of confinement. To be sure,
it was not possible to make meaningful comparisons of
long- and short-term patients on all measures because of the
relatively small sample sizes. The instruments which lent
themselves most readily to such comparisons were those
with repeated measures: the Twenty Statements Test and
the semantic differentials.

"Who am I" and length of confinement. To study the
relationship between length of confinement and patient responses to the Twenty Statements Test, German and
American patient groups were combined and were then divided into two groups: patients confined less than three
months ($N = 52$) and those confined over two years
($N = 70$).

These two groups responded differently to only one of
the seven categories of the Twenty Statements Test, and
even this difference was slight. There was a slightly greater
tendency ($P < .06$) for the short-term patients to characterize themselves in terms of physical attributes (e.g., "I'm
tall"; "I have blue eyes"). This could, of course, merely
reflect a tendency on the part of the long-term group to give
fewer responses. To test this possibility, the two groups
were compared for the number of responses each individual
made. There was a slightly greater tendency for the short-
term group to make more (eleven to twenty) statements,
while the long-term group made one to five statements or
six to ten statements ($P < .05$).

Semantic differentials and length of confinement. An
analysis of variance compared responses of short-termers
and long-termers to all six dimensions of all five concepts of
the semantic differentials. The results were striking. Only
the ratings of *Insane Person* differed significantly. These
ratings differed on four dimensions: activity ($P < .001$);
certainty ($P < .01$); understandability ($P < .05$); and predictability ($P < .05$). In every case, the long-term groups
rated *Insane Person* more positively on these dimensions
than did the short-term groups. The two patient groups did

not differ in their self-evaluations, i.e., their ratings of the concept *Me*.

Thus, the expected differences between the two groups' self-evaluations did not appear, but the long-term group did tend to rate *Insane Person* more positively on the semantic differentials. These ratings could reflect the long-termers' greater acceptance of the status of mental patients, or they could reflect merely a greater familiarity with the reality of insanity and a rejection of the negative stereotypes of the insane. As noted previously, the latter possibility is not unlikely, given the staff groups' relative rejection of negative stereotypes, noted in chapter 1. It is quite probable that "professional socialization" in this sense develops in both staff and patients in the hospital. Both become more tolerant and accepting of the mentally ill (at least on paper) than they had been as laymen.

According to the conversion approach, long-term patients should define themselves as mentally ill and identify with the mentally ill more than short-term patients. All of the empirical studies cited above failed to demonstrate these differences. To be sure, they lacked longitudinal data; they merely compared the responses of long-term patients to those of short-term patients. Strictly speaking, then, these studies can tell us little about the *process* of institutionalization. To talk authoritatively about the changes that occur during institutionalization, one would have to collect extensive longitudinal data. These difficulties notwithstanding, it is significant that these cross-sectional studies failed to demonstrate "conversion" in a majority of either long-term or short-term patients. If a significant number of patients had really accepted "the hospital's view of them," this should have appeared in their statements about themselves and about other patients. In fact, statements purporting such a view were extremely rare. Since findings like these raise serious questions about the conversion approach, it behooves us to examine this approach more closely.

Conversion vs. Adjustment

Goffman outlines four different modes of adjustment to

total institutions: (1) situational withdrawal; (2) intransigence; (3) colonization; and (4) conversion (1961:61–62). Only in conversion does the inmate fully accept the institution's definitions of him. In the other modes the inmate is able to insulate himself to some extent against the institution's efforts to redefine him. Thus, although institutionalized inmates may exist in any one of the four modes, only the conversion mode involves an actual acceptance of the official line, i.e., the inmate comes to believe that he possesses some characteristic (e.g., mental illness, criminal tendencies) and that, because of this characteristic, he belongs in the institution. Goffman argues (1961:64) that most inmates do not pursue any one mode very far but rather adopt "a somewhat opportunistic combination of secondary adjustments, conversion, colonization, and loyalty to the inmate group." Thus, when discussing the characteristics of total institutions, Goffman suggests that most inmates are *not* converted (1961:61–66). However, in his analysis of mental hospitals (1961:127–69, 375–86), he consistently implies that the institutionalization of mental patients consists in converting them, i.e., the patients must come to accept the hospital's definition of them. This emphasis was exemplified in the quotations from Goffman, above (1961:150, 155, 165, 376).

Goffman's analysis apparently contains an internal inconsistency. In the first part of his discussion he argues that most inmates of total institutions are not converted. In the second part of his analysis he repeatedly suggests that institutionalization of mental patients involves converting them. This contradiction has not been obvious to other researchers because of the vagueness of Goffman's discussion. Goffman never plainly states that patients come to believe they are mentally ill. Instead, he says that patients must accept the hospital's view of them (1961:155). Although he consistently implies that the hospital's view of the patients is that they are sick and in need of treatment (1961:376–72, 150), he never explicitly spells out what the hospital's view is or how this view is manifested by the patients once they have accepted it. Goffman's vagueness and the internal inconsistency in his argument have produced some confusion in research on institutionalization. The following section presents a case in point.

Conversion vs. Impression Management

Braginsky et al. found that, given certain inductions, long-term mental patients would modulate their behavior in order to remain in the hospital (1966, 1967, 1969). These authors interpreted their results as refuting Goffman's theory (1961) of institutionalization. They argued that if, according to Goffman's theory, their subjects had been institutionalized, they would have "thought of themselves as mentally ill." Braginsky et al. then cited studies that indicated that patients do not generally define themselves as mentally ill (Joint Commission on Mental Illness and Health 1961; Levinson and Gallagher 1964). From this Braginsky concluded that (a) long-term patients do not "really" think of themselves as mentally ill; (b) therefore, their long-term patients' responses do not reflect an actual *change* in self-concept but rather manipulation of impression management; and (c) therefore, Goffman's theory is inaccurate; the hospital's role in institutionalization is "omissive" rather than "commissive"; patients remain in the hospital due to a logical *choice* and implement this choice by manipulating their behavior (1966, 1967).

Braginsky et al. have thus taken one mode of institutional life, that of "conversion," and made it into the sine qua non of Goffman's theory. This is unfortunate because Goffman explicitly states that inmates seldom pursue one mode very far (1961:65). Braginsky's interpretation is understandable, however, given, as we saw above, Goffman's almost exclusive emphasis on conversion in his subsequent discussion of mental hospitals (1961:125–386).

Having correctly established that most mental patients do not appear to have been "converted" but rather engage in impression management, Braginsky et al. then proceed to argue that this represents a "logical," "rational," and "voluntary" decision on the patients' part to remain in the hospital. The hospital has allegedly played only an "omissive" role in affecting this decision. This leap in Braginsky's reasoning represents a non sequitur and obscures the issue: it negates the role of the institution in *producing* the patient's desire to remain in the hospital. There is mounting evidence that role expectations in institutional settings do indeed produce measurable changes in the behavior and perceptions of individuals. This evidence comes from diverse sources. First, researchers who have had themselves admitted as patients in order to study mental hospitals consistently report the same "commissive" effects of degradation and depersonalization that are described in Goffman's theory (Goldman et al. 1970; Rosenhan 1973; Hemprich and Kisker 1968). Second, it is common knowledge that one of the avowed tasks of behavior modificationists working on mental-hospital wards is to eliminate "symptomatic" behavior that has been produced by inadvertent reinforcement from the staff (Ullmann and Krasner 1969). Third, numerous researchers, including Braginsky and associates (1969), have shown that social context and expectations can produce "symptomatic" behavior (Fontana and Klein 1958; Levitz and Ullmann 1969). Fourth, studies have also shown that role expectations can drastically affect the behavior of noninstitutionalized individuals. For example, experiments have shown that role expectations can produce "brighter" and "duller" students (Rosenthal and Jacobson 1958); induce subjects to (unconsciously) fulfill experimenters' expectations (Orne 1962); induce subjects to give a "heart patient" ostensibly lethal shocks (Milgram 1965); and turn college students into "brutal prison guards" and "rebellious inmates" (Zimbardo 1972). The subjects in these studies were "normal" and were allegedly less susceptible to suggestion than individuals who end up in mental hospitals (Wing 1962; Braginsky et al. 1969; Zusman 1973). If role expectations could drastically alter these persons' behavior, there is every reason to believe that the expectations of mental-hospital staff could obtain similar results with mental patients.

Finally, it is an established fact that, the longer a patient stays in the hospital, the less chance he has of getting out and staying out (Strauss and Carpenter 1972; Paul 1969). Given all this evidence, it seems unreasonable to assume that "patient susceptibility" or "family ties on the outside" or some other variable external to the hospital could completely account for institutionalization. It also seems unreasonable to assume that these external variables are themselves unaffected by what happens to the patient in the hospital. In this regard, it is noteworthy that, after arguing against any "commissive" effects of the hospital, Braginsky et al. (1969:172) concede that they were "utterly unable" to answer the question of what determines whether the individual will choose the particular path of institutionalization as a means of withdrawing from society.

Although the Braginsky studies contain some extremely valuable information, the logic of their argument is faulty. The crucial flaw in Braginsky's argument lies in his failure to distinguish between patients' "presenting" themselves as mentally ill (i.e., engaging in "symptomatic" behavior) and "defining" themselves as mentally ill. Patients may engage in extremely symptomatic behavior, but they seldom overtly define themselves as mentally ill. This was true of all the empirical studies reviewed above, including Braginsky's own (1969). This does not necessarily mean, however, that the old-timers in the hospital have not been taught the role of chronic patient by the institution. Indeed, part of the chronic-patient role apparently consists of face-saving rationalizations for the patient's presence in the hospital (e.g., "I have a physical illness"; "I'm here for a rest"; "I was framed"). The tendency of mental patients to rationalize their presence in the hospital has been described by Goffman (1961) and was a frequent element in interviews conducted by the present researcher as well. However, while the patient is denying he is mentally ill, he may simultaneously engage in behaviors (both within and without the hospital) that ensure his continuing status as a mental patient. That is to say, he may "present" himself as mentally ill (in interviews and tests as well as in gross behaviors) while simultaneously claiming he is sane. It is thus quite possible that the behaviors measured by Braginsky's interviews and tests (1969) and by those of the other studies do in fact reflect the patients' institutionalization: patient behavior is altered by long-term confinement, but these alternations do not consist of obvious deterioration or verbalized identification with the "insane." Rather, institutionalization consists of an *acceptance* of the status of mental patients, and this acceptance is reflected in symptomatic behavior both inside and outside the hospital but not necessarily in patients' self-evaluations. This acceptance, in turn, has been conditioned by multifarious factors, including the hospital's view and treatment of the patient, the loss of extra-institutional roles, and the real changes wrought in one's life by entry into the status of "mental patient" (Lamy 1966; Steadman and Cocozza 1974:135; Dinitz et al. 1961; Greenly 1972; Honigfeld and Gillis 1967).

It thus appears that the results reviewed above, as well as those of Braginsky et al., are consistent with Goffman's *general* theory of institutionalization: the longer the stay, the more likely it is that the inmate will make an opportunistic adjustment to the institution. The inmate will not, however, necessarily accept the institution's definition of him (1961:61–66). It was Goffman's subsequent emphasis on changes in self-concept (1961:127–69, 375–76) that led Braginsky et al. to interpret their results as refuting Goffman. The vagueness of this part of Goffman's theory has apparently led several researchers to draw some very questionable conclusions about the nature of mental hospitals. Given this vagueness, one may well ask what the theory is worth and how it can be empirically tested.

Behavior vs. Self-Concept

Numerous studies, including a bicultural comparison, have apparently failed to demonstrate the changes in institutionalized patients' self-concepts that would be predicted by Goffman's theory. Empirical studies that have successfully studied the effects of long-term confinement have generally ignored changes in self-concept as an index of institutionalization. They have instead operationalized (usually implicitly) the concept of institutionalization. For example, although Wing begins his article (1962) with a synopsis of Goffman's theory, he quickly shifts to a more behavioral definition of institutionalization. He states explicitly that institutionalization consists of changes in attitudes and behavior. One of his indices of institutionalization was a checklist, filled out by the charge nurse, that consisted of observable behaviors, e.g., socially embarrassing

behavior and social withdrawal. Wing's general definition of institutionalization was also behavioral. He defined institutionalization as "an apathetic attitude toward
leaving the hospital." Such a definition obviated the problem of defining and measuring "self-concept" and consequently allowed Wing to conclude that the symptoms of
institutionalization increased with length of stay.

The approach taken by Shiloh (1971) is similar. Like
Wing, he begins his article with a very positive review of
Goffman's theory but then (implicitly) shifts to a more behavioral definition of institutionalization. If a patient expressed no desire to leave the hospital, he was considered
institutionalized. Shiloh's results suggest, however, that institutionalized patients have undergone a certain type of
conversion. For example, in contrast to noninstitutionalized patients, they accepted locked wards for new
patients as desirable, they spoke more favorably about
the hospital, and they stressed the recreational and custodial aspects of the hospital rather than its rehabilitative aspects. The institutionalized patients could also better
describe what a "good patient" was like than what a good
nurse or doctor was like. Their good patient, of course, was
one who adjusted to hospital life and made no trouble.
From these results Shiloh concluded that, on the whole,
institutionalized patients viewed the hospital not as a hospital but rather as an "old-folks home." These patients' conversion, then, consisted more of an *acceptance* of hospital
life and of themselves as inmates rather than in coming to
believe that they were mentally ill. Like Wing, Shiloh thus
shifted his emphasis away from a concern with true conversion (i.e., accepting the institution's definition of one's self)
to a more behavioral and operational conception of institutionalization.

Other researchers have taken a similar approach. Barton
(1959), for example, describes institutionalization in terms
of behavioral symptoms (e.g., posture, gait, withdrawal).
He argues that the institutionalization of mental patients
derives from the tendency of all human beings to adjust to
adverse circumstances in the most secure and comfortable
way possible. Miller (1961) similarly focuses on the behavioral symptoms of institutionalization. Although he uses

clinical labels in describing the modes of institutionalization, he argues that these modes occur independently of
diagnostic categories. In their discussion of "chronicity,"
Sommer and Whitney (1961) also stress the behavioral manifestations of institutionalization (e.g., passivity, dependence, blind acceptance of authority). They define the
chronic patient as one who has become so dependent on the
hospital that he can no longer manage on the outside.
Chronic patients are to be differentiated from chronic
schizophrenics, many of whom, because their illnesses
have stabilized, can live on the outside.

Since they tend to view institutionalization as an *adjustment* to hospital life, these studies are all consistent with
Braginsky's portrait of the hospital as a nonmedical "resort" for people who have few options in the outside world
(1969), and they are also consistent with Goffman's initial
description of the "opportunistic" adjustment made by
most inmates (1961:61–66) but not with his suggestion that
mental patients must come to take the hospital's view of
them (1961:155). The evidence thus suggests two things.
First, institutionalization does not necessarily consist of
convincing the patient he is insane. At least, empirical
studies have consistently failed to demonstrate this process. Second, the studies that have successfully demonstrated the effects of long-term confinement have generally
focused on behavioral symptoms. This does not mean,
however, that the self-concepts of mental patients do not
change over time. Although chronic patients may not state
that they are mentally ill, it seems reasonable to assume
that people will feel differently about themselves when they
move from an active role in society to the role of a chronic
mental patient.

It is interesting to note that data on nonhospitalized
schizophrenics in Puerto Rico support this inference.
Rogler and Hollingshead found that all but one of their
sample denied they were mentally ill; however, these individuals tended to suspect that they might be becoming
mentally ill, and they admitted to being more "nervous"
than did a matched sample of controls (1965:221–25).

The fact that empirical research has failed to demonstrate
the proposed changes in self-concept raises the question of

the utility of "self-concept" as a research tool. Although studies of self-concept have certainly contributed to our understanding of psychology generally, they may be less useful in the study of mental patients. To be sure, it is difficult to define what anybody "really" thinks of himself, because people's feelings about themselves change with context. But most people show some consistency in their responses, and it thus can be worthwhile to explore how they talk about themselves or respond to paper-and-pencil tests concerning themselves. Mental patients, however, are in a special situation. They know that their subjective feelings are under constant scrutiny, and they know that this scrutiny helps determine their fate. It is thus not surprising that mental patients modulate their behavior on tests and interviews depending on what they perceive to be the purpose of the test (Braginsky et al. 1966; Fontana and Klein 1968). They have experienced this type of probing before, and have seen its effects. Given the mental patient's special situation, it may not be a meaningful question to ask what he "really" thinks of himself. His responses will not necessarily match his actual feelings at the moment, and, in any case, both feelings and responses will tend to vary with context. At times the patient may feel good about himself; at other times, bad. Some may suspect at times that they are insane and yet not admit these suspicions. At other times things may be going well, and they consequently feel very healthy; even so, they may still fear leaving the safety of the hospital and, as a result, do poorly during a staff evaluation. Patients, like anyone else, are also capable of deceiving themselves. They may inwardly suspect they are insane yet ward off confrontation with these feelings by rationalizing their presence in the hospital and denying that they are mentally ill.

It thus appears that it is difficult to define exactly what a patient thinks of his condition at any one time, and it may be that this is not an empirically useful question. In view of these considerations, it is understandable that so many studies of institutionalization have focused on behavioral manifestations rather than on hypothetical changes in self-concept.

The fact that empirical studies of mental patients have

consistently failed to reveal the expected differences in self-concept suggests that the part of conversion theory that emphasizes such changes is not very useful in empirical research. All of these studies did, however, support the notion that institutionalization involves an acceptance of institutional life and utilization of its recreational rather than its rehabilitative aspects. In these studies, then, institutionalization, in its simplest form, becomes a lack of desire to leave on the part of the patient. The authors of these studies have (implicitly) dropped the self-concept part of conversion theory and shifted to more behavioral concepts. This seems more appropriate to the empirical study of institutionalization.

On the other hand, the conversion approach has made a major impact on the study of institutions, and it is significant that the two empirical studies reviewed in detail above (Wing 1962; Shiloh 1971) began with very positive reviews of Goffman (1961). It is evident that Goffman's approach has been a powerful force in sensitizing researchers to the phenomenon of institutionalization. Perhaps Goffman's "quasi-phenomenological" approach was necessary for this task; perhaps it is necessary that the reader be made to "feel what it's like to be a mental patient" in order to be sensitized. After the reader is sensitized, he can then proceed to develop concepts and strategies that are more useful in the empirical study of institutionalization.

Institutionalization in Germany and America

The data from the present study do not allow specific conclusions concerning possible differences in the processes of institutionalization in German and American hospitals. I would, however, like to offer some of my overall impressions at this juncture. According to my personal observations, the institutionalization of mental patients seems to occur through the same process in Germany and America: patients are inadvertently rewarded for a cooperative, compliant adjustment to hospital life without simultaneous rewards for appropriate, extra-institutional behaviors and without successful development of meaningful options in the outside world. This process has gained increasing recognition in America and, to some degree, in Germany, and it is largely because it has been recognized that experimental rehabilitation programs have been instituted and that attempts are being made to transfer patients to outpatient care and halfway houses (Gottesfeld 1976).

Although the same basic process apparently underlies institutionalization in the two countries, there are important differences. As we saw in chapter 2, German patients possess more biological conceptions of illness and stronger extra-institutional definitions of self. They may thus be better insulated against the hospital's view and treatment of them. On the other hand, the Germans may be less aware of how conformity and impression management can influence staff decisions, and, being less aware, they may make fewer efforts to influence these decisions by modulating their own behavior. In contrast, American patients may be more aware of the possibilities of impression management, but, consequently, they may also be more likely to overcompensate, to become unctuous in their efforts to attract staff attention, or to use impression management in order to remain in the hospital (Braginsky et al. 1969).

Alternatively, the American patient may recognize the institutional requirements and the "game" he must play to get out, but the recognition itself can cause such anger and frustration that he rebels against the institution, thus ensuring his continued confinement and possibly launching him on a deviant career as a chronic troublemaker (Goffman 1961:62).

The position of the German patient, therefore, is not necessarily superior to that of the American patient. Rather, the German patient faces a different problem: if he learns his diagnosis, directly or indirectly, or if he otherwise begins to suspect that he is *geisteskrank* (insane), then, by his own cultural conceptions, there is no real hope of cure. The American patient, on the other hand, agrees with his staff that there is always hope. With personal effort and the proper guidance he can be cured. This assumption, which puts a tremendous responsibility on the patient, frequently involves moral condemnation by the staff and consequent guilt on the part of the patient. The possibility of cure (like the possibility of social mobility in America) is thus a two-sided coin. On the one side it allows for hope, but on the other side it condemns failure. It is due to this conception of personal responsibility and willpower that the American patient, more than the German patient, faces a peculiar dilemma. If he accepts the institutional definition of himself as mentally ill, it may become increasingly difficult to maintain (or reconstruct) healthy extra-institutional definitions of self. If he does not accept the institution's definition of him, and indeed rebels against it, his rebellious behavior itself may become his symptom and ensure his continued confinement.

Conclusion

From the evidence marshaled above, it appears that patient behavior is altered by long-term confinement, but these alterations do not consist of obvious deterioration or verbalized identification with the "insane." Rather, institutionalization consists of an *acceptance* of the status of "mental patient," and this acceptance is conditioned by multifarious factors, including symptomatology, the hospital's view and treatment of the patient, and the loss of extra-institutional roles (Strauss and Carpenter 1972; Pasamanick et al. 1967; Davis et al. 1972). In the next chapter we shall examine another tenet of the social-role camp: that psychiatric diagnoses are somewhat arbitrary and are used as a means of social control.

4   Clinical Universalism: Some Problems and Questions

In the preceding chapters we have examined evidence that supported a social-role approach to mental disorders. We saw that mental-health professionals in Germany and America share certain conceptions of mental illness with their publics. We also saw that mental patients in both countries hold views similar to their publics and their professionals. These same basic assumptions and conceptions were reflected in the patients' statements concerning symptomatology and coping behavior within the hospital. In chapter 3 it was argued that long-term confinement in mental hospitals tends to produce chronicity but that this "institutional syndrome" consists more in patients' becoming apathetic about leaving than in coming to believe that they are really mentally ill.

It is time now to examine the major tenets of the school that opposes the social-role approach: *clinical universalism*. The argument here is not intended as a refutation or a defense of either the social-role approach or clinical universalism. Rather it seeks to demonstrate that, although the universalist argument possesses some validity, the implications and tone of the argument can be extremely misleading. In the first part of this chapter I will argue that the signs and symptoms of mental disorders are much less objectively verifiable and much more ambiguous than is implied by the universalists. In the second part I will contend that psychiatric labels can be somewhat arbitrary, that they do imply certain treatments, and that some of these treatments can be deleterious to the patient's welfare. I will not attempt to do justice to the full scope and variation within each school. Instead, the emphasis will be on analyzing some fallacies and implicit assumptions that have given rise to misunderstandings and have plagued the debate between the two schools. The evidence adduced below in support of the social-role approach consists primarily of empirical research published in psychiatric journals. As we shall see, many top research psychiatrists now recognize the need for a modification of the present clinical approach (Carpenter et al. 1977; Engel 1977; Strauss et al., 1977).

In contrast to the social-role approach, clinical universalism asserts that, except for superficial variation in content, psychiatric disorders are fundamentally the same throughout the world. E. B. Forster, a psychiatrist with considerable experience in Ghana, summarizes this view:

> Psychiatric syndromes or reactions, by and large, are similar in all races throughout the world. The mental reactions seen in our African patients can be diagnosed according to Western textbook standards. The basic illness and reaction types are the same. Environmental, constitutional and tribal cultural background merely modify the symptom constellation. Basically, the disorders of thinking, feeling, willing and knowing are the same (1962:35).

The transcultural psychiatrist Alexander Leighton offers a similar, if more amusing, testimony from his interviews with native healers in Nigeria:

> On one occasion a healer said to me, through an interpreter: "This man came here three months ago full of delusions and hallucinations; now he is free of them." I said, "What do these words 'hallucination' and 'delusion' mean? I don't understand." I asked this question thinking, of course, of the problems of cultural relativity in a culture where practices such as witchcraft, which in the West would be considered delusional, are accepted. The native healer scratched his head and looked a bit puzzled at this question and then he said: "Well, when this man came here he was standing right where you see him now and thought he was in Abeokuta" (which is about thirty miles away), "he thought I was his uncle and he thought God was speaking to him from the clouds. Now I don't know what you call that in the United States, but here we consider that these are hallucinations and delusions!" (Ciba Foundation Symposium 1965:23).

E. L. Margetts, also a psychiatrist with broad cross-cultural experience, states the universalist position even more positively:

The more I listen to the discussion of transcultural psychiatry, the more I am coming to believe that perhaps there is no such thing ... [we have not] learned a great deal about it since the time of Kraepelin. As far as I am concerned, psychiatry is the same all around the world: the signs and symptoms of mental diseases are the same, the diagnoses are the same and there is probably just as much possession syndrome in England as there is in equatorial Africa (Ciba Foundation Symposium 1965:24).

Not all critics of the social-role approach possess a clinical background. In a recent critique of Scheff's labeling theory (1966) of mental disorders, the sociologist Walter Gove asserted that a majority of relevant empirical studies support the medical approach rather than the social-role approach to mental disorders (1975b). Although Gove admits that mental institutions have produced a great deal of "secondary deviance," he believes that the medical model best explains what "typically happens" (Gove 1975b:245; Gove and Howell 1974:80). Similarly, in response to Rosenhan's charge (1973) that the sane cannot be reliably distinguished from the insane, critics from various specialties rebutted that psychiatric illnesses are indeed valid scientific taxa that can be diagnosed reliably (Spitzer 1975; Millon 1975; Weiner 1975; Kety 1974).

In a recent paper, the anthropologist Jane Murphy reaffirmed this position and suggested that Western psychiatric labels are valid transculturally (1976:1019):

These cross-cultural investigations suggest that relativism has been exaggerated by labeling theorists and that in widely different cultural and environmental situations sanity appears to be distinguishable from insanity by cues that are very similar to those used in the Western world.

In fact, since the time of Ruth Benedict's early work (1934), a great deal of cross-cultural evidence has accumulated that tends to support the central thesis of clinical universalism: *the major psychoses do seem to be found universally*. To be sure, cultural conditioning appears to cause considerable variation in the content of symptoms (Yap 1951; Schooler and Caudill 1964) and may even cause substantial variation in the frequency of different disorders, although there is some controversy on this latter point

(Eaton and Weil 1953; Draguns and Phillips 1972; Murphy 1976). This variation notwithstanding, it appears that conditions resembling our categories of "schizophrenia" and "affective psychoses" are recognized and considered aberrant in every society (Yap 1965; Lambo 1965; Edgerton 1966; Eaton and Weil 1953; Kiev 1972). I thus do not seek to refute this fundamental tenet of clinical universalism. Rather, in this part of the analysis I will attempt to demonstrate that, although the psychoses may exist universally, their diagnosis is not a simple matter. Experts do not always agree on who is psychotic or which type of disorder is present. Finally, I will present further evidence to support the social-role hypotheses: diagnostic labels are in part a cultural product, are sometimes arbitrary, and are used as a means of social control.

The Unreliability of Diagnosis

Under certain conditions, psychiatric diagnosis can be quite reliable. A study of the biological and adoptive relatives of schizophrenic adoptees (Kety et al. 1971; Kety 1974) demonstrated the following: (a) three raters independently reached a high level of agreement on who among the index and control groups was schizophrenic; (b) those diagnosed as schizophrenic were much more likely to have biological relatives who were schizophrenic. Kety (1974:960) concluded from these results that insanity (and, in particular, "schizophrenia") can be distinguished from sanity quite readily. The researchers in this case were trained to use the same criteria in diagnosing the primary data, which consisted of summaries of psychiatric interviews *written by one member of the team.* There does not seem to be any doubt that with such training and standardization a high degree of reliability in diagnosis can be reached. These, however, are not conditions that obtain in the millions of diagnostic judgments that are made each year in the United States. The physicians who make such judgments come from different training backgrounds and often subscribe to very different theories of mental illness. Furthermore, they are frequently overburdened with case loads and administrative duties. It is in conditions such as these that a "presumption of illness" may occur, i.e., those

inducted into the psychiatric system are *presumed* ill. T
is a contention, of course, of several advocates of
social-role approach (Scheff 1966; Rosenhan 1973).

Definitive empirical studies of this problem have yet to
be done, so it is impossible at this point to know for certain
how much "presumption of illness" does occur in American hospitals. Lacking such studies, we shall turn to some
cross-national investigations of diagnosis that bear directly
on this question.

Recent cross-national studies have demonstrated consistent differences in diagnostic tendencies (Katz et al.
1969; Rawnsley 1967; Cooper et al. 1969; Gurland et al.
1969; see also note 2 to chapter 2). The most extensive
comparisons have been made between British and American psychiatrists (Kendell et al. 1971), and the results are
especially interesting because many of the possible sources
of variation in diagnosis were controlled. Because the two
groups possessed a common cultural and language background and because they all viewed the same videotapes of
patient interviews, it was expected that cross-national variation would be minimized. In fact, some surprising differences emerged. Three patterns of diagnostic agreement
or disagreement tended to emerge (Kendell et al.
1971:126–27). First, British and American psychiatrists
agreed substantially in their major diagnosis of patients who
exhibited symptoms typical of the classical stereotypes;
agreement was poor, however, both between and within
countries, on the subtype of depression or schizophrenia
involved. The second group of patients presented a mixture
of schizophrenic and affective symptoms. A majority of
psychiatrists in both groups diagnosed these patients as
schizophrenic, but among those who gave another diagnosis a significantly greater number of British psychiatrists (20–34 percent) diagnosed affective psychosis. A third
group of patients caused serious disagreement. The American viewers of the videotapes tended predominantly to diagnose schizophrenia (69–85 percent), while the British
shunned this category (2–7 percent). This glaring difference
was not due merely to semantics. That is, the psychiatrists
were not seeing the same symptoms but labeling them differently; rather, *psychiatrists were actually perceiving dif-*

ferent symptoms in the patients' behavior. One patient, for example, was rated by 67 percent of the American psychiatrists as having delusions, by 63 percent as showing passivity, and by 58 percent as showing thought disorder (Kendell et al. 1971:129). The corresponding percentages for the British raters were 12 percent, 8 percent, and 5 percent.

These results tended to replicate the findings of an earlier study. Katz et al. (1969) had also found that psychiatrists generally agreed on the major diagnosis for patients who exhibited the classic textbook symptoms of schizophrenia or depression. More ambiguous cases, however, gave rise to alarming differences. Diagnoses made by a group of American psychiatrists on one patient (an aspiring actress) were almost equally distributed among the major diagnostic categories of psychosis, neurosis, and personality disorder. Furthermore, although one-third of the Americans diagnosed this woman as schizophrenic, *none* of the British psychiatrists did so. As in the preceding study, these differences were not merely semantic but, instead, arose from the viewers' actually perceiving different symptoms in the patient's behavior. In discussing these results, Kendell et al. (1971) point out that, because schizophrenia lacks demonstrable organic pathology, there is no way of verifying who is right when experts disagree. For all practical purposes, then, the disorder consists of the symptoms, and, if experts disagree on symptoms, even the presence of the disorder is questionable (Kendell et al. 1971:128):

> In consequence, though one may discuss whose concept of schizophrenia is more useful, or closer to Bleuler's original description, one cannot meaningfully discuss which is right, for we have no external criterion to appeal to—no morbid anatomy, no etiological agent, no biochemical or physiological anomaly.

These authors further caution that their results have serious implications for psychiatry, for if experts cannot agree on a major diagnosis, they can neither define research populations nor share information effectively with colleagues. In short, without a reliable taxonomy, a *science* of psychiatry becomes impossible (1971:128).

Diagnostic Labels and Social Control

There are other lessons to be learned from the British-American comparisons. First, in ambiguous cases, diagnosis appears to be more of a cultural product than a matter of objectively identifying a syndrome. Kendell et al. make this point rather strongly (1971:129):

> Although ... no concept of schizophrenia can be either right or wrong, it does seem, at least to a European observer, that the diagnosis is now made so freely on the east coast of the United States that it is losing much of its original meaning and is approaching the point at which it becomes a synonym for functional mental illness. Seven of the eight patients in this study were diagnosed as schizophrenic by over two thirds of the American psychiatrists, although between them they presented a variety of different symptoms and problems. Similarly, in a recent random sample of 192 patients below the age of 60 admitted to public mental hospitals in New York City, 82% of those with nonorganic conditions were diagnosed as schizophrenic by the hospital psychiatrists. But doubtless the situation looks very different when seen through North American eyes and any major changes in either the British or American concepts of schizophrenia will probably occur only after, and as a consequence of, therapeutic innovations or biochemical or physiological discoveries. Changes currently taking place in the American concept of mania illustrate this quite well. The diagnosis of mania was in danger of disappearing, at least in New York, until lithium salts were introduced as a specific treatment of manic illnesses. The interest aroused by this new drug has, however, caused patients who five years ago would have been regarded as schizophrenics to be diagnosed now as manic depressives in order that they may be given lithium salts.

A more recent study of diagnosis also tends to support the view that social factors greatly influence psychiatric labeling. Cohen et al. (1975) found that the discharge diagnosis was much less serious that the intake summary in about 15 percent of their target population. Interviews with the psychiatrists responsible revealed that diagnosis had been changed not because of any change in symptoms but because of social considerations. Psychiatrists listed the following reasons for changing diagnoses: (1) protecting adolescents; (2) prejudice of school officials; (3) occupational stigma; (4) social biases; (5) possibility of insurance companies' using information. The patients most likely to be protected in this way were employed males. The housewife category was the least represented in the protected group (particularly black women). Presumably, this bias reflects the psychiatrists' greater desire to protect working males from social stigma and job discrimination. Cohen and his associates concluded that social factors are frequently crucial determinants of diagnosis and thus of patients' careers. They also point out that their data raise serious questions as to the validity of diagnostic statistics around the country (1975:427). Apparently, both cross-national and intracultural studies of diagnosis tend to support the social-role thesis that psychiatric labels are, in part, a cultural product and are therefore somewhat arbitrary.[1]

These studies of diagnosis may also support another tenet of the social-role approach. Being somewhat arbitrary and a cultural product, diagnostic labels may function as devices for social control. Thomas Szasz (1960, 1970) is probably the best-known spokesman for this position, but numerous other authors have also stressed this point (Stanton and Schwarz 1941; Goffman 1961; Scheff 1966, 1967; Braginsky et al. 1969; Rosenhan 1973). These authors propose (with varying emphases) that many people are labeled mentally ill in our society merely because they pose a problem for society. They are people who are old, indigent, jobless, and have few interpersonal ties or roots. They are people who have problems in "getting along" and "fitting in." In Szasz's words, they have "problems in living" (1960).

There is some evidence to support this view. Several authors have noted that state mental hospitals in America tend to serve the same populations as the old almshouses of the nineteenth century (Stearns and Ullman 1949; Miller 1965, 1967; Braginsky et al. 1969). Stearns and Ullman's investigation of one such institution over a period of ninety-four years revealed that the inmates had not changed much—only society's label for them had (1949). Before, they were merely helpless and poor; now they had become mental patients. In the nineteenth century the inmates were largely jobless, homeless, indigent people with no real ties or opportunities in the outside world. On examining the contemporary patient population, the authors concluded that most of the patients were there for the same reasons: they were neither acutely nor chronically psychotic, but they lacked family, friends, and the skills and connections that would enable them to cope in the outside world.

A large follow-up study of former mental patients in California yielded similar results. Miller (1967) found that 85 percent of her sample stemmed from the lower classes. Only 48 percent were married, compared to the California average of 85 percent. They had few family connections, liitle education, and generally were "important to nobody." In five years, 71 percent of the sample had been readmitted to the hospital. These people simply had nowhere else to go.

In their study of social class and mental illness, Hollingshead and Redlich (1958) reported similar findings. They found that the lower classes in America show a much higher prevalence of mental illness than the upper classes. But when "prevalence" was broken down into its component parts, it was found that, while the incidence of new cases of psychosis was 43 percent higher in the lower class than in the upper, *the tendency to remain in mental hospitals was 380 percent higher in the lower classes*. Unless one claims that, because of some unknown biological cause, the diseases of the lower classes differ in their development from those of the upper classes, this difference between initial incidence and tendency to remain in the hospital can be explained in terms of the inferior treatment the lower classes receive, their lack of legal and financial resources, and their lack of options in the outside world. In the same vein, Braginsky et al. (1969) proposed that many such patients manipulate their behavior in order to *remain* in the hospital. Although there is controversy over the percentage of patients who do this (Price 1973), authors tend to agree that for some patients, at least, the hospital represents a "last resort"; they simply have nowhere else to go (Braginsky et al. 1969; Shiloh 1971; Miller 1965, 1967).

The analysis of *Baxstrom* patients mentioned in chapter 1

also supports this view of mental hospitals. Steadman and Cocozza found that social support was crucial in determining whether these patients (diagnosed as criminally insane) would be released to the community (1974:135):

> In examining the relative effects of these variables, it was found that the single most important factor for the release of these patients was the presence of an interested family in the community. This finding is very similar to Greenley's (1972) that family desires are closely related to the timing of release. It is also the strongest example encountered in our work of the importance of social factors for understanding what happens to mental patients, an issue we raised in Chapter 1. More important for their release than how well they were mentally, how well they were adjusting within the civil hospital or any other consideration, including those related to their dangerousness, was whether there was an interested family.

Feldman, in evaluating community mental health centers (1974:25), flatly states that one of the major reasons mental hospitals continue to exist is that there are thousands of people living in them who have nowhere else to go. Fotrell and Majumder (1975) estimate that such patients may compose as much as 40 percent of the total. Talbott (1974) found that 60 percent of admissions to the Meyer-Manhattan Psychiatric Center in New York were readmissions. In evaluating 100 of these readmissions, he and his team judged that 84 of them could have been prevented had better services been available (e.g., vocational rehabilitation, follow-up treatment, involvement with patients' families). These studies, then, are consistent with the view of institutionalization developed in chapter 3: patients adjust to a residential existence both because the hospital environment encourages them to do so and because they lack meaningful options in the outside world.

This view of the state mental hospital is also consistent with the data and discussion in chapter 1. There we saw that, compared to Germans, Americans tend to believe that a person can maintain or restore mental health by manipulating his environment and exerting personal effort. It was also argued that these conceptions are consistent with the general American emphasis on self-reliance: people are expected to exert personal effort and manipulate their environment in order to succeed on their own; if they do not, they are considered failures and are scorned. Such a value orientation seems very consistent indeed with the argument of the social-role theorists outlined above: America, unable to face squarely the results of its extreme emphasis on self-reliance, may induct many of its disadvantaged persons into the state-supported mental-health system. Here, at least, they receive food, clothing, and shelter.

Although I have no specific data on the subject, I would suspect that Germany is less "socially darwinistic" than America. The Germans seem to be more socialistic in their policies, and they possess national health insurance. Coupled with a higher rate of employment (particularly for unskilled workers), these conditions may tend to minimize the number of people who are in the "rootless and helpless" category; that is, if familial roles remain stronger in Germany and economic conditions are better, fewer people are left without family ties and jobs. For these reasons, I suspect that mental hospitals function less in Germany as dumping grounds for societal rejects, and I believe that patients and staff in that country show an awareness of this by viewing the hospital as a "hospital." The hospital may not function as much as a last resort for the helpless in Germany because Germany has fewer people who are rootless and helpless. If this is true, it must influence the way patients are treated and, consequently, their symptomatology. Consistent with this hypothesis are the results of chapter 2, which indicated that German patients tend to maintain better extra-institutional definitions of self.

There is some evidence to support these inferences. Taube and Redick (1973), for example, argue that rehabilitation efforts in America are hampered by the fact that the United States is not a full-employment society. Former mental patients have great difficulty competing for jobs in conditions of labor surplus. In contrast, countries with labor shortages (e.g., the U.S.S.R.) tend to have very successful rehabilitation programs. Aviram and Segal (1973) have shown that American attempts to close mental hospitals and treat patients in the community have often resulted in the patients' becoming even more isolated and ghettoized. "Nice" people do not want halfway houses and outreach centers in their neighborhoods, and former patients are frequently forced to live in isolated and depressing conditions. Such conditions, of course, contribute to a high rate of recidivism, i.e., the hospital becomes a revolving door, as noted above (Talbott 1974; Feldman 1974; Greenblatt 1974; National Institute of Mental Health 1971). Similarly, competition and rivalry among various agencies hinder effective coordination and delivery of health care in America. In Europe, national health plans allow "sectorization," in which a variety of coordinated mental-health programs become available to *all* people in a given geographic area (Gittelman 1974).

This critical view of the American mental-health system also receives indirect support from the cross-national studies of diagnoses reviewed earlier. It will be remembered that three types of patients emerged in the British-American comparisons conducted by Kendell et al. (1971): (1) psychiatrists generally agreed on the major diagnosis for patients with classic textbook symptoms; (2) patients with mixed affective schizophrenic symptoms caused considerable disagreement; (3) some patients were diagnosed completely differently by the two groups of psychiatrists, with Americans favoring schizophrenia and the British favoring nonpsychotic categories. The authors remarked that the problems raised by the second group are well known and "manageable" (1971:127), that is, American psychiatrists have a broader concept of schizophrenia, and the British have a correspondingly broader concept of affective disorders. The third group of patients, however, raises more serious problems, and the authors comment on this at length (1971:127):

> But disagreements as glaring as this have serious implications. Diagnoses are the most important of all our technical terms because they are the means by which we identify the subject matter of most of our research. They identify the types of patients who received the drug we were assessing, or whose family dynamics or sodium metabolism we were studying. If these terms are used by different groups of psychiatrists in widely differing ways, the two will, at best, fail to

communicate with each other, and may well actively mislead one another.

For a certain percentage of patients, there is thus little agreement on whether they are psychotic or not. The patients in this third group, then, may represent the population discussed by social-role authors, i.e., the people who have "problems" and who present a problem to society but who are neither psychotic nor neurotic in any objectively verifiable sense. The results of the British-American comparisons suggest that there may be many such people in American institutions who are routinely labeled "schizophrenic." Two questions arise: (1) What percentage of patients enter or remain in the American mental-health system primarily because of problems in living? (2) Should these people even be "patients" in psychiatric facilities? These questions, of course, are subject to further empirical investigation, but, as noted above, some evidence suggests that the percentage is considerable and that alternatives to psychiatric treatment should be sought (Fotrell and Majumder 1975; Talbott 1974; Feldman 1974; Braginsky et al. 1969).

In a now classic work, Parsons (1951) predicted that, increasingly, medical definitions in America would be expanded to include various types of deviance. What was formerly considered criminal, reprehensible, or merely a nuisance would become "medical problems" and would therefore be subject to social control through medical intervention. Examples of this process would include drug and alcohol use (Szasz 1975), homosexuality (recently "declassified"), and old age. Formerly, these phenomena were "deviant," but they were not considered psychiatric problems. Now, as a result of the expansion of definitions, these people "have" psychiatric problems. Indeed, an official of a large state mental hospital told the present author that about 30 percent of their inpatient population were really geriatric cases. There was just "no other place to put them."

The evidence examined in this section thus suggests the following. First, social-role theorists are correct in asserting that psychiatric diagnoses can be quite arbitrary and that they can function as a means of social control. Second, the central tenet of clinical universalism is also correct: there *are* people who would probably be diagnosed transculturally as psychotic. These are the people who exhibit classic textbook symptoms, and it seems logical to assume that it is this population upon which the clinical-universalist argument rests. Third, it appears that there are also people who are diagnosed as schizophrenic in America who would *not* be diagnosed transculturally as psychotic. These are the people with "problems in living" who present a problem to society. Psychiatric labels function to induct these people into the "mental-health" system, where they can be processed and treated. Logically, these are the cases that would best support the social-role approach to mental disorders. The following questions are raised: (1) What percentage of American patients belong in either the universal group or the problems-in-living group? and (2) Is it possible that the problems-in-living group suffers from their treatment in psychiatric facilities? To answer the latter question is the purpose of the next section.

Effects of Labeling and Treatment

Although the arguments of clinical universalists vary in their emphasis, they generally imply that the negative effects of labeling and ensuing treatment are negligible. In their view, mental disorders are diseases, they have biological causes, and the symptoms of the disease itself determine the societal reaction rather than the converse. There is something reassuring in this view, of course, for it implies that our own society's reaction to mental disorders is justified. If the signs and symptoms of mental disorders are universal, and if societal reactions to these symptoms are similar throughout the world, then the American method of dealing with mental patients must be "all right." This tone is clearly evident in the following passage (Murphy 1976:1025):

> If one defines intolerance of mental illness as the use of confinement, restraint, or exclusion from the community (or allowing people to confine or exclude themselves), there does not appear to be a great deal of difference between Western and

non-Western groups in intolerance of the mentally ill. Furthermore, there seems to be little that is distinctively cultural in the attitudes and actions directed toward the mentally ill, except in such matters as that an abandoned anthill could not be used as an asylum in the arctic or a barred igloo in the tropics. There is apparently a common range of possible responses to the mentally ill person, and the portion of the range brought to bear regarding a particular person is determined more by the nature of his behavior than by a pre-existing cultural set to respond in a uniform way to whatever is labeled mental illness.

There is, of course, some validity in these remarks. Some symptoms probably do elicit similar reactions throughout the world: the physically dangerous are restrained and the ludicrous are ridiculed. This type of generalization, however, implies a universality of symptoms and treatment that, as we have seen, does not exist. Although the exact percentage is uncertain, the evidence examined above suggested that a sizable proportion of American "schizophrenics" would not be so labeled in Britain (or in Europe, for that matter). This pattern may be changing, however, because the popularity of lithium salts as an antipsychotic medication has increased the popularity of affective disorder as a diagnosis (Kendell et al. 1971:129). Furthermore, there seems to be one group of "schizophrenic" American patients who would not even be diagnosed as psychotic (Kendell et al. 1971:127). This diagnostic variation is not merely semantic. It has grave implications for the patient, for different diagnoses tend to imply different treatments. Patients diagnosed as psychotic are generally treated quite differently from those who are not. For example, patients diagnosed as psychotic are more frequently (1) hospitalized, (2) involuntarily committed, (3) held not legally responsible, (4) given major tranquilizers or lithium salts, and (5) treated with shock. Thus, in implying a universality of symptoms and treatment that does not exist, clinical universalists tend to obfuscate major legal, moral, and scientific problems. They imply that the attack on institutional psychiatry by social-role theorists is unjustified because symptoms and societies' reactions to symptoms are universal (Murphy 1976:1025).

In the first part of this chapter I argued that the perception of symptoms, and thus the diagnostic label assigned, can vary considerably cross-culturally. I will now seek to demonstrate that societal reactions vary substantially, that the different reactions implied by different diagnoses can have markedly different effects on the patient, and, in particular, that the decision to hospitalize a patient may be deleterious to his welfare because the hospital environment itself may tend to produce chronicity.

Phillipe Pinel (1745–1826) is often credited with having been the first to experiment with modifications in hospital treatment of mental patients (1962). He introduced more humane treatment methods at the Bicêtre and the Salpêtrière in Paris and noticed a marked improvement in the behavior of his patients. Such "moral" treatment changed the treatment emphasis from one of confinement, force, and physical restraint to one of psychological and milieu therapy. Methods of moral treatment were subsequently undertaken in England with even more pronounced results (Tuke 1813; Conolly 1856). In spite of its success, moral treatment was almost completely abandoned toward the end of the nineteenth century. The return to more physical and coercive methods was accompanied by a return to therapeutic nihilism. In 1893 the German psychiatrist Emil Kraepelin published his classic textbook of psychiatry, which argued that certain mental illnesses, including dementia praecox (now called schizophrenia), were chronic and degenerative (Kraepelin 1902). Patients with these diseases were doomed to inevitable deterioration; the environment could have no effect on their symptomatology.

Around the turn of the century, another German psychiatrist, Eugen Bleuler, repudiated the nihilism of Kraepelin. In his classic work on schizophrenia, Bleuler argued that schizophrenic symptomatology was in large measure determined by environmental events (Bleuler 1950:349):

> Almost the totality of the heretofore described symptomatology of dementia praecox is a secondary, in a certain sense, an accidental one. Therefore, the disease may remain symptomless for a long time. Whether a particularly chronic schizophrenic is able to work peacefully today or wanders about and quarrels with everyone, whether he is neat and clean or

smears himself—that is, the nature of the symptoms— depends mainly on past or present events and not directly on the disease. Some affectively charged experience releases a hallucinatory agitated state. A transfer to another hospital may bring about the disappearance of the same hallucinations.

Studies since Bleuler's time have consistently supported his thesis. Unlocked wards and the replacement of harsh physical methods with psychological-milieu methods of treatment tended to reduce both overt symptomatology and deterioration in inpatient populations (Jones 1953; Bell 1955; Rees and Glatt 1955).

More recently, researchers have concentrated on describing specific aspects of the hospital environment that tend to produce chronicity. Although their emphases vary, researchers generally agree that prolonged confinement in mental hospitals tends to produce an "institutional syndrome." As we saw in chapter 3, this syndrome consists of generalized apathy, lack of initiative, indifference toward discharge, occasional aggressive outbursts, deterioration of personal habits, and resignation. These symptoms become confused with the symptoms of the disorder, and a researcher can really disentangle them only when the institutional symptoms clear up as a result of intensive rehabilitation (Wing 1962; Barton 1959; Miller 1961; Sommer and Witney 1961; Martin 1955).

Some authors argue that institutionalization consists of actually convincing the patient he is mentally ill; in so convincing the patient the hospital inducts him into a sick role, which ensures a good adjustment on the inside but virtually precludes a readjustment to life on the outside (Goffman 1961; Zusman 1973). Although, as noted in chapter 3, there is disagreement on whether most mental patients actually do come to believe they are mentally ill (Braginsky et al. 1969; Price, 1973), students of institutionalization generally agree that the syndrome consists of the symptoms cited above and that both patient susceptibility *and* the institutional environment contribute to this syndrome.

Empirical results have consistently supported this view. Numerous studies have related poor prognosis (i.e., rehospitalization or continued hospitalization) to marital status, socioeconomic class, social relations, and length of previous hospitalization(s). As might be expected, patients who were currently married, came from higher social classes, had good social networks, and had experienced shorter hospitalization(s) had a better prognosis (see Paul 1969 for a review of the literature). More importantly, length of hospitalization seems to correlate with a poor prognosis even when other variables are partialed out of the relationship (Honigfeld and Gillis 1967). To be sure, such correlations are subject to multiple interpretations. It is possible that "sicker" people (i.e., those with more severe symptoms) are likely to be hospitalized for longer periods of time and are also more likely to be rehospitalized (i.e., they have a poor prognosis). This is, of course, how traditional clinicians would explain such correlations, and, as noted above, it is a view often implied by clinical universalists.

The results of an extensive comparison of home care with hospital care, however, suggested that symptoms alone cannot account for the correlation between length of hospitalization and poor prognosis. In what has come to be an extremely influential study, Pasamanick et al. (1967) found that patients treated at home had a significantly better prognosis than matched controls treated in the hospital. These results thus suggested that the hospital experience itself helped produce chronicity. Indeed, it was results like these that initiated a movement in several states to reduce inpatient populations and treat patients on an outpatient basis (National Institute of Mental Health 1971:1; Davis et al. 1972; Feldman 1974).

The results of a more recent study of outcome in schizophrenia also support the notion that case outcome is affected by several variables, including social relations and length of hospitalization. In a highly sophisticated study of 142 patients, Strauss and Carpenter (1972) found that their results did not support the view that schizophrenia has a predictable outcome. Areas of outcome dysfunction (work, symptoms, social relations and nonhospitalization) were found to operate as open systems; that is, they were partially interrelated, but each was also affected by variables specific to it alone. The authors also found that outcome for schizophrenic patients overlapped with other diagnoses (i.e., the other areas of outcome dysfunction were relatively independent of diagnosis). This was true even when Kurt Schneider's narrow criteria for schizophrenia (widely used in Germany) were utilized to classify patients. The authors concluded that their findings (1972:745) challenge the utility of outcome as a validating criterion for the concept of schizophrenia or as a criterion used to differentiate schizophrenia from patients hospitalized with other severe functional mental disorders. In sum, the findings challenge the notion that schizophrenia (or any diagnosis) has a predictable outcome. Instead, outcome seemed to be determined by an interaction of the four areas of dysfunction: work, symptoms, social relations, and length of hospitalization.

In addition to the damaging effects of institutionalization, there is mounting evidence that anti-psychotic medications may have serious side effects. A recent report in the *American Journal of Psychiatry* points up some alarming facts (Carpenter et al. 1977). First, administration of neuroleptics (major tranquilizers) is automatic and immediate for most patients. Treatment with these drugs often precedes and even precludes a diagnostic evaluation. Millions of patients receive neuroleptics as the only important component of their treatment. Second, recent studies indicate that these drugs may have serious negative effects for some patients. Many patients should at least have the benefit of an adequate trial without drugs, but most patients do not get such a trial (Davis 1975; Gardos and Cole 1976). From previous studies and their own results, Carpenter et al. conclude the following (1977:19):

> In any case, in an illness with so many paradoxes, we raise the possibility that antipsychotic medication may make some schizophrenic patients more vulnerable to future relapse than would be the case in the natural course of their illness. Thus, as with tardive dyskinesia, we may have a situation where neuroleptics increase the risk for subsequent illness but must be maintained to prevent this risk from becoming manifest. Insofar as the psychotic break contains potential for helping the patient alter pathological conflicts within himself and

establish a more adaptive equilibrium with his environment, our present-day practice of immediate and massive pharmacological intervention may be exacting a price in terms of producing "recovered" patients with greater rigidity of character structure who are less able to cope with subsequent life stresses.

All this suggests that labels and their ensuing treatments can markedly influence outcome, particularly when the treatment includes hospitalization and drugs. The labels "schizophrenia" and "institutional syndrome" clearly imply different treatments, and whether this treatment consists of incarceration in a custodial institution or home care supervised by a public-health nurse definitely affects the patient's prognosis. Contrary to the claims of the clinical universalists, then, labels and societal reactions are not "universal" and therefore reliably predictable. They vary substantially, and they can have powerful effects on a person's fate. These effects can be benign or deleterious.

In addition to institutionalization as a negative effect of treatment, social-role advocates propose that psychiatric labeling stigmatizes a person and reduces his life-chances. Gove and Fain (1973) have recently disputed this claim, citing evidence from a study of 429 patients from a Washington state hospital. Former patients were asked one year after hospitalization whether their hospitalization had done them "any good" or whether it had harmed them in any way. Over 70 percent cited positive effects; only 14 percent responded negatively. The authors concluded from these results that mental patients *generally* do not suffer from stigma and discrimination. To be sure, on paper-and-pencil tests the average layman evinces extremely negative attitudes toward mental patients. But, Gove and Fain argue (1973:500), in real-life situations people "apparently act in a socially desirable (humane) fashion (which is the reverse of the way social desirability is assumed to interact with verbal responses and actual behavior)."

This conclusion, though certainly heartening, does not seem justified by the data Gove and Fain present, for we cannot conclude for certain that the patients in their sample suffered no discrimination, and we certainly cannot conclude that mental patients generally do not suffer from stigma. We only know that a majority of particular patients, from this particular geographic region, reported positive rather than negative effects of their hospitalization. In interpreting Gove and Fain's results, we should also remember that the interviews they report were part of a very large pilot study of a progressive new treatment program in a state hospital. It is quite possible that the interviewers were seen by patients as representative of the hospital system (and perhaps even of the program) and were thus not considered a proper audience for complaints about hospitalization. More importantly, Gove and Fain tell us virtually nothing about the actual situations of these patients. What were their social, economic, and employment opportunities before and after hospitalization? What did their employers and acquaintances think about their hospitalization? Answers to these questions would certainly help tie the authors' data to more general statements about stigma. As it stands, we cannot conclude that people generally act in "humane" ways toward mental patients. Indeed, there is considerable evidence to the contrary.

The first line of such evidence concerns the closing of mental hospitals. Greenblatt (1974) cites resistance from the community as a primary force operating against the phasing-out of mental hospitals. Middle-class people do not welcome the release of "unattractive" patients into their midst, and they react violently against plans for halfway houses and outreach centers in their neighborhoods. In their study of the exclusion of the mentally ill, Aviram and Segal (1973) cite numerous examples of intense community rejection of such facilities. In fact, they argue that economic reasons alone cannot explain the ghettoization of the mentally ill, many of whom move to slum areas because their efforts to live in other neighborhoods are blocked (Aviram and Segal 1973:129):

> In one such case a man wanted to buy a house for his family and four expatients and was threatened by other people in the neighborhood. He gave up the idea and said: "I know I am entitled to live there but that is not the issue. My wife and kids, that's what's most important" (*The Vista Press*, Dec. 1, 1971).

The authors conclude from their study that the establishment of alternative-care facilities in communities has been resisted in various ways, including zoning laws, city ordinances and regulations, and informal approaches, such as neighborhood pressures and bureaucratic maneuvering. This rejection, coupled with a lack of adequate funds, leads to a ghettoization of mental patients, which in turn contributes to a high rate of recidivism.

The *Baxstrom* decision reviewed in chapter 1 also testifies that extreme stigma attaches to the mental-illness label (Steadman and Cocozza 1974). In 1966, in the case of *Baxstrom* v. *Herold*, the Supreme Court ruled that patients in hospitals for the criminally insane were entitled to judicial review after their criminal sentences had expired. These reviews would determine whether the patients were mentally ill and, if so, whether they could be transferred to civil mental hospitals. Rather than provide myriad reviews at tremendous expense, the State of New York transferred 967 "criminally insane" patients to civil hospitals. This caused "extreme anxiety among both hospital staffs and the surrounding communities" (1974:186). Staff and public did not want nor, they claimed, were they equipped to handle such dangerous patients.

A four year follow-up of these patients after their transfers revealed that these fears were totally unjustified. While they were in civil hospitals, about 15 percent exhibited assaultive behavior (presumably a modest percentage when compared to other confinement situations, like prisons or even urban high schools). Approximately 25 percent of the *Baxstrom* patients were discharged to the community. Of the 98 patients (in the study sample) who were discharged, only about 20 percent were subsequently arrested, and half of these were convicted. Most of the convictions were for minor nuisances, such as public intoxication, disorderly conduct, or vagrancy. In only 2 of the 98 cases was there a conviction for a "violent" crime (namely, grand larceny and robbery).

It must be emphasized that these 967 patients had been judged "criminally insane" and for years were consistently denied discharge because they were considered "extremely dangerous." Steadman and Cocozza therefore concluded that the popular image of the mentally ill as dangerous is very seriously distorted and that society's treatment of the "criminally insane" is unwarranted and unjust.

There is also some experimental evidence that stigma attaches to psychiatric labels and facilities. Rosenhan (1973) had students ask for directions in a medical school: half the time they were to ask for the psychiatric ward, and half the time for the department of internal medicine. The reactions to the two inquiries were markedly different. In the first case, many of those questioned averted their eyes, barely answered, and continued walking. In the second case, most of the respondents were extremely helpful. These data, though certainly not conclusive, definitely suggest that real people in real situations react in a prejudiced way toward psychiatric labels.

To study the effects and the amount of stigma against former mental patients, we need more empirical work in real situations rather than more interviews or paper-and-pencil tests. For example, one might wonder why, if no discrimination is planned, so many personnel departments have questions concerning psychiatric treatment on their application forms.Moreover, one might ask why, if no discrimination exists, people go to such lengths to conceal psychiatric histories. (Why, for example, is Alcoholics Anonymous anonymous?) We know that a psychiatric history can be disastrous to some careers (e.g., the career of Senator Eagleton), but we do not know the variables that determine such reactions. One way to approach this problem would be to establish test cases, much as the NAACP has done in its fight against racial discrimination. Experimental confederates would apply for various jobs. On half the applications they would admit to a psychiatric history; on the other half they would not. Only by such experiments in real situations can we begin to establish how much discrimination occurs in everyday life.

One final question to be considered is whether former mental patients suffer discrimination because psychiatric labels carry stigma or because so many chronic patients are poor and helpless. In reality, I believe that these phenomena are only theoretically separable. As noted above, the poor have a much greater tendency to remain in the psychiatric system once they have entered it. The poor are thus more likely to be in psychiatric facilities—including community mental-health centers as well as custodial institutions. Because of inadequate funds, their own initial poverty, and community rejection of progressive programs, mental patients are forced to live in depressing slum conditions. These conditions in turn contribute to a self-fulfilling prophecy: mental patients are disheveled and unattractive in appearance. This image then reinforces the public stereotype of the mentally ill and further increases their rejection and reduces their opportunities. As discussed in chapter 1, American values are hostile to those who are not strong and self-reliant. American conceptions assume that those who are poor, helpless, or mentally ill must somehow be responsible for their fate, and this is even further reason to shun them. In this way, I believe that stigma, poverty, helplessness, and continuing psychiatric treatment interact to keep people helpless and in the psychiatric system, and it is this interaction that determines the degree to which the American mental-health system functions to control the disadvantaged.

Conclusion

In this chapter I have argued that, although the major psychoses are found universally, their diagnosis is not always a simple matter. Psychiatric diagnoses can be arbitrary, and they can have deleterious effects on the patient's welfare. Finally, we saw that American psychiatrists tended to diagnose as "schizophrenic" some patients who would be classified as "neurotic" or as having "problems in living" by British psychiatrists. This raised the questions: What percentage of American patients would fall in this category? and Should they even be treated psychiatrically? Both are, potentially, empirically testable questions.

In contrast, the debate between the clinical-universalist and social-role theorists has seldom centered on testable questions and for that reason has often tended to generate more heat than light. Recent exchanges between Scheff and his critics exemplify this failing. Scheff and his critics agree that both approaches, the clinical and the social-role, find some support in empirical studies (Scheff 1974; Murphy

1976; Gove 1975b:245; Chauncey 1975; Gove and Howell 1974:80). For these researchers the question to debate has become: Which approach can best account for the majority of the evidence and which best explains "what typically happens"? (Gove 1975b:245). Unfortunately, these questions are not stated in a testable form and are thus empirically meaningless. Consequently, the two camps can (and do) continue to debate which model "best accounts for the majority of available evidence" (Gove 1975b; Chauncey 1975; Scheff 1975). Since all the combatants agree that *some* secondary deviance is produced by labeling and treatment, the more meaningful questions to pose are How *much* of the symptomatology and recidivism of chronic patients is produced by the societal reaction, and how can it be reduced? Studies like those reviewed above have begun to provide answers (Pasamanick et al. 1967; Strauss and Carpenter 1972; Steadman and Cocozza 1974; Talbot 1974; Cohen et al. 1975; Carpenter et al. 1977). Such studies have important policy as well as theoretical implications, and they could serve as models in this respect for researchers in the area. In contrast, further debate over semantics or over which model "best accounts for the evidence" can serve only to distract attention from the empirically meaningful issues and consequently to impede further progress. In the next chapter I will explore some of the issues that have divided the two schools and will propose a model that allows evidence for both approaches to be encompassed in one framework.

5   Illness or Social Roles:
             A False Dichotomy

In chapter 4 I argued that social-role theorists are correct in asserting that psychiatric labeling is to some degree arbitrary and that it can have damaging effects on people. In this chapter I will attempt to demonstrate (1) that the social-role and clinical-universalist schools are actually using different populations to buttress their arguments; (2) that both schools tend to dichotomize between biology and learning; and (3) that a repudiation of this dichotomy and a more comprehensive conception of "role" allows a synthesis of the two approaches.

Different Populations

The reader will remember from Chapter 4 that three types of patients emerged in comparisons of British with American psychiatrists. For the first type there was substantial agreement on the major diagnosis; these patients exhibited classic textbook symptoms. The second type elicited majority agreement on the major diagnosis but wide variation among those dissenting. For both of these types there was little agreement on the subtype within the major diagnostic category. The third type of patient elicited almost total disagreement between British and American psychiatrists. In interpreting these results, the authors emphasized that the major disagreements resulted from psychiatrists' actually perceiving different symptoms rather than from semantic differences in classification (Katz et al. 1969; Kendall et al. 1971). I argued that these results suggest that "symptomatic" behaviors can be interpreted quite differently and that these different interpretations can lead to different societal reactions and treatment. Several other lines of evidence tend to support this view.

In extensive retrospective analyses of outcome, Miller

(1965, 1967) found that younger patients with shorter periods of hospitalization, from higher social classes, and with specific jobs and family roles to return to had a better prognosis. Aside from length of hospitalization, bizarre behavior was the variable most consistently related to rehospitalization across all living conditions. Miller found, however, a curvilinear relationship between severity of symptomatic behavior and the reactions of family members. Certain mildly distressing behaviors were tolerated by all. At the other end of the scale, certain radically deviant behaviors were nearly always associated with rehospitalization. A middle range of behaviors, however, was associated with tolerance of deviance. That is, if significant others were distressed, rehospitalization occurred; if they were not, community tenure continued.

In discussing recognition and labeling of the mentally ill from a cross-cultural perspective, Edgerton (1969) proposed a similar scheme. He argued that markedly deviant behavior, if both chronic and sufficiently bizarre, would probably result in recognition and labeling in any culture. However, most symptoms are not both chronic and extremely bizarre. Cases that are not both chronic and markedly bizarre but are sufficiently disruptive to cause a societal reaction are the subject of "negotiation." That is to say, it is in the equivocal middle-range cases that sociocultural factors play their strongest role in determining outcome. Factors like the social status of the deviant, the role expectations awaiting him after the acute phase passes, and the family's wishes regarding his fate can be decisive in middle-range cases.

Edgerton's analysis (1969) of cross-cultural evidence is thus consistent with Strauss and Carpenter's findings. As noted in chapter 4, Strauss and Carpenter (1972) found that outcome was not generally predictable from diagnosis and that the different areas of outcome dysfunction (work, symptoms, social relations, and nonhospitalization) could influence one another but could also be partially independent. That is, these areas interacted as open systems; they influenced one another but were also influenced by variables specific to them alone. The partial independence of these systems was exemplified by cases in which hospitalization as a measure of outcome was independent of the other areas because of the family's ability (or lack thereof) to care for the patient, the presence or absence of job opportunities, or because of legal requirements that the patient remain hospitalized. All of these variables, including hospitalization, could be independent of the patient's clinical status.

The partial independence of these outcome areas seems to parallel the negotiation process discussed by Edgerton (1969). Negotiation in the recognition and labeling of middle-range cases involved many of the same variables as the interaction of the open systems described by Strauss and Carpenter (1972). Some of these variables were the status of the deviant, the nature of the deviance, the desires of the family, the deviant's performance of work and family roles, and the availability of these roles after the acute phase had passed.

These two studies suggest an interactional view of outcome: several variables—including length of hospitalization, social relations, work, and symptoms—interact to determine outcome. From this interactional view, it follows that sociocultural factors will have their greatest impact on outcome in middle-range cases. These are the cases without obvious, stereotyped, and chronic symptomatology. It is in these cases that diagnosis and treatment are not cut and dried, and it is therefore in these cases that social factors can have their greatest influence. The more ambiguous the case, the more a social factor like family status can become decisive. For example, in an ambiguous case, high family status could prevent hospitalization in a custodial institution, and this in turn could prevent the patient from developing chronic institutional syndrome. This type of process is, of course, exactly what the social-role theorists emphasize. In their view, outcome (and symptoms) are not independent of social factors like social class and employment opportunities. Evidently, then, that part of the social-role argument that stresses an interactional view is supported by the studies of outcome cited above.

If my argument is valid, it is the middle-range cases that best support the social-role approach to mental disorders. These are the cases where social factors have their greatest impact on outcome. By the same logic, cases with more obvious, stereotyped, and chronic symptoms best support the clinical-universalist approach. Individuals with florid, stereotyped symptoms would probably elicit essentially similar societal reactions throughout the world (Murphy 1976). It remains an empirical question, however, what percentage of mental patients in the United States fall within the "ambiguous" as opposed to the "stereotyped" group (most patients, of course, will tend to vary in this regard over time). One way to attack the question would be to investigate what percentage of patients diagnosed as psychotic in this country would not be similarly diagnosed in other countries. If a large discrepancy were found, one would want to ask whether these people should be diagnosed as psychotic or whether they should even be treated in psychiatric facilities. The answers to these questions have serious implications for national mental-health policies.

Apparently, the social-role theorists and the clinical universalists use different phenomena to buttress their arguments. Social-role authors concentrate on describing the negotiational and interactional *processes* that help to determine outcome in middle-range cases, while clinical universalists tend to cite cases with unambiguous, classic, textbook *symptoms* to support their claims for universality. It would seem that much of the debate between these two schools could be obviated if it were recognized that these are different populations *and* different foci.

Biology vs. Social Learning

I have just suggested that part of the controversy between clinical universalists and social-role theorists arises from the fact that they are really concentrating on different phenomena in different populations. I will now seek to demonstrate that both schools tend to dichotomize between biology and social learning. I will argue, finally, that a rejection of this dichotomy allows a synthesis between the two approaches.

In stressing that mental disorders are diseases with universal signs and symptoms, clinical universalists generally tend to separate the biological state of the organism from its social learning. Although authors vary in their tendency to do this, it seems to be a pervasive characteristic of that school. The following examples illustrate this tendency.

In its *Diagnostic and Statistical Manual* (1968), the American Psychiatric Association posits two types of depression: the *reactive*, which is a reaction to traumatic environmental events, and the *endogenous*, which is genetic in origin and is independent of environmental events. Thus, the reactive is a response to the environment (i.e., it is "learned"), while the endogenous is genetically determined and is thus not "learned." As we saw in chapter 2, German psychiatry tends to dichotomize *all* the psychoses in this way. Recent experimental and clinical evidence does not, however, support such a dichotomy; instead, affective disorders seem to develop from an interaction of genetic and environmental factors (Akiskal and McKinney 1973:21).

Many American clinicians support a dichotomous view of other mental disorders as well. For example, the transcultural psychiatrist Ari Kiev proposes that psychological stress does not cause mental disorders (1972). Rather, the person's genetic predisposition to a disorder impairs his ability to cope. His inability to cope then produces psychological stress. In this scheme, stress is thus an effect rather than a cause of mental disorders (Kiev 1972:5). Rimland (1969) assumes a similar position. He argues that there is no cogent evidence that social learning can help cause mental disorders. In his view, genes predispose the individual to a certain type of breakdown. Meehl (1962:837) makes the same point when he states that "schizophrenia, while its content is learned, is fundamentally a neurological disease of genetic origin."

Some critics of the social-role approach argue explicitly that schizophrenic symptoms are independent of role-playing. Chauncey (1975:249) claims that case studies make it "obvious" that symptoms and social roles are independent phenomena. He does not, however, explicate what is so "obvious." Rosenbaum (1969) makes this point even more explicitly. He claims that viewing schizophrenic symptoms as social roles is tantamount to characterizing schizophrenics as malingerers and schizophrenia as a "put-on." This statement clearly misconstrues the concept of "social role," for it implies that a person "puts on" his role behavior much as a malingerer consciously pretends to be sick.

Although some clinical universalists do not affirm this dichotomy directly, their arguments imply it. Consider, for example, the following quotation (Murphy 1976:1027): "Rather than being simply violations of the social norms of particular groups, as labeling theory suggests, symptoms of mental illness are manifestations of a type of affliction shared by virtually all mankind." This statement implies that symptoms are universal "afflictions" and are therefore somehow independent of a person's norm violations or other role behavior.

It appears, then, that clinical universalism implies that symptoms are independent of social learning and social roles. Curiously enough, the social-role theorists also imply this dichotomy, for they either reject the whole concept of symptom (because they argue that abnormal behaviors are social roles, not diseases), or they view the acquisition of the deviant social role as independent of the individual's biology. For example, Scheff, in the flow-chart depicting his theory (1966:100), proposes that initial deviance springs from diverse causes, "biological, psychological, and social." This initial deviance is then molded, through the expectations of others, into the stereotyped roles of insanity. These are "learned" roles; that is, Scheff implies in this scheme that social learning of this kind is separate from the biological causes of the deviance and the ongoing biological processes of the individual. Social learning is somehow laminated onto the psychobiological factors.

Numerous other social-role researchers also separate biology from learning. For example, Levitz and Ullmann (1969) have shown that operant conditioning can produce indications of disturbed thinking in normal college students. Other experiments have shown that chronic schizophrenics can increase or decrease their reaction time depending on what they perceive to be the purpose of the test (reaction time has long been considered, of all schizophrenic deficits, the most resistent to alteration [Fontana et al. 1968; Fontana and Klein 1968]). These authors conclude that their results support the theory that the mental hospital inadvertently reinforces the symptomatic behavior of patients (Goffman 1961; Ullmann and Krasner 1969). All these authors thus contend that symptomatic behaviors are *learned* in the hospital.

The position assumed by Braginsky et al. (1969) is similar. They found that mental patients modulate their behavior (i.e., show more or less "pathology") depending on what they perceive to be the purpose of the interview. They thus argue that neither pathology nor "institutional syndrome" is necessary to explain patient behavior. Rather, patient behavior is the result of learned rational choices based on the inferior options existing for the patients outside the hospital (Braginsky et al. 1969).

Apparently, leading social-role theorists also imply a dichotomy between biology and social roles. In doing so, they commit the same error as the clinical universalists. Both groups assume that a person cannot learn "real" pathology; both assume that "symptoms" are not altered by learning. I shall argue, below, that biology, and thus "real" pathology, is really inseparable from a person's social roles.

In separating social learning and biology, both schools participate in two hoary and long invalidated dichotomies: instinct vs. learning and mind vs. body. It is only by invalidating these dichotomies, and by seeing biology as a result of and interactant with social conditioning, that the present impasse between the two schools can be overcome. The arguments against these dichotomies are numerous and varied (e.g., Beach 1955; Lehrman 1970; Engel 1977; Madsen 1974). Here I must necessarily simplify and present only the most pertinent.

Roles

Social roles are inseparable from organic processes for the following reasons. First, as Goffman (1959) and Sarbin and Allen (1968) have noted, normal social roles are not "put on," in the sense that they are voluntary. They are essentially "inaccessible" to the individual's scrutiny or analysis, and, in this sense, they are unconscious. For example, a physician does not need to remind herself constantly that she is a physician and that she must treat her patients differently from the way she treats her husband, her colleagues, and her dog. Different behaviors for these different situations come naturally for her as she locates herself in each instance within a broad field of role expectations provided by the culture. She does not "put on" being a physician any more than she "puts on" being a woman, a mother, and a wife. She *is* these things, and her "identity" or "self" consists in her particular style and execution of these roles at any given moment.

Second, roles involve the total organism; they are not independent of its biology. While a person's genetic makeup (genotype) does not change during his lifetime, a person's biology results from the interaction between genotype and environment. Culturally conditioned behavior is thus only theoretically separable from biology. The executive's ulcer and the perspiration on the surgeon's brow are not "just" somatic responses, nor are they "put on." They are biological manifestations of deeply ingrained social roles. Numerous studies suggest that certain cultural and ethnic milieus predispose people to particular psychosomatic reactions. These reactions are not the result of hypochondria or malingering; they are not "put on;" they include such real somatic complaints as ulcers, allergies, migraine headaches, cerebral vascular accidents, and even death as the result of magic (Zborowski 1952; Mechanic 1972; Cannon 1942; Ecker 1954). Moreover, it has been demonstrated in countless settings that role expectations mobilize organic systems of the body. Additional evidence is now accumulating from the use of operant conditioning, biofeedback (Brown 1974), and the scientific study of various yogic practices (Wallace and Benson 1972). Through these techniques people have learned to control such "autonomic" responses as blood pressure, galvanic skin response, pulse rate, brain waves, and peristaltic contractions. Strictly speaking, then, an individual's biology is inseparable from his social behavior. A person's biology *interacts* with his social experience; each influences the other. I suggested above, however, that both clinicians and social-role theorists continue to dichotomize between biology and social roles. To clarify these issues and to bridge the gulf between the clinical universalists and the social-role theorists, it is necessary to examine some basic concepts more closely. In the following pages I will argue that the controversy between the social-role theorists and the universalists stems largely from faulty conceptions of biological causation and faulty conceptions of social roles. I shall discuss genetic causation first. What is this evidence for the genetic determination of mental disorders? The most extensive and sophisticated research on genetic causation of mental disorders has been done on schizophrenia in twins and adoptees.

Genetic Causation

Monozygotic (identical) twins are genetically identical; consequently, if schizophrenia is simply an inherited genetic trait, both twins should either have it or not have it. The early studies (e.g., Kallmann 1953) showed rates of concordance between twins as high as 86 percent. In other words, if one twin was schizophrenic, the probability was very great that the other would be also. These results supported the view that an inherited genetic trait caused schizophrenia and that the environment played little or no role. Rosenthal (1969) and Kringlen (1969) have demonstrated that these early correlations were spuriously inflated by sampling errors and faulty methodology. In a very careful study of schizophrenic twins in Norway, Kringlen (1969:32) found the following rates of concordance based on hospitalized cases of schizophrenia and schizophreniform psychoses: monozygotic twins, 25 percent; dizygotic (fraternal) twins, same sex, 7 percent. When Kringlen utilized his personal knowledge of the nonhospitalized cases, the rates increased to 38 and 10 percent, respectively. His findings tend to support the view that though genes are involved in the etiology of schizophrenia they are not necessarily decisive. Environment apparently plays a role too. Theoretically, the environmental factors could be psychosocial, physical-chemical, or both. The evidence is still inconclusive.

Dohrenwend (1975) has carefully reviewed three bodies of evidence for psychosocial factors causing mental disorders. The first consists of epidemiological studies of "true" prevalence of mental disorders (i.e., both treated and untreated cases). These studies consistently reveal significant correlations between poverty and higher rates of mental disorders. Such correlations, however, are subject to multiple interpretations. It is also possible, for example, that persons genetically predisposed to mental disorders "drift" into poverty due to their inability to cope. Dohrenwend proposes a research strategy that would attempt to resolve this question, but the problems of implementing such research are formidable.

Second, Dohrenwend analyzes the literature on individual reactions to extremely stressful situations, e.g., combat fatigue or "shell shock." There seems to be no doubt that extreme stress can cause temporary mental breakdowns. Some authors have questioned, however, whether these temporary breakdowns are really comparable to what are commonly termed the "functional" mental disorders. Third, more ordinary stressful events (e.g., losing one's job) tend to correlate with mental disorders, but again it is not clear whether these events are causes or symptoms of the mental disorder; the evidence from this body of literature is even more equivocal than that on extremely stressful situations. Thus, after reviewing a very large number of studies on psychosocial factors, Dohrenwend was forced to conclude that the results are inconclusive. He notes with irony that biogenetic studies provide the strongest (though indirect) support for psychosocial factors in the etiology of mental disorders: inheritance cannot explain all the variation; consequently, environmental factors (possibly psychosocial) must also be involved. More recent biogenetic studies also support this view.

In studying the relatives of adult schizophrenics who had been adopted in infancy, one research team found that the biological relatives of schizophrenics showed significantly more pathology than the families who had raised the schizophrenics (Kety et al. 1971). Similarly, 76 adopted offspring of schizophrenic parents were compared with a matched sample of 67 adopted controls. The rate of diagnosis of schizophrenia-spectrum disorders for the index group was 31.6 percent, compared to 17.8 percent for the controls. The evidence from all these studies strongly supports the theory that heredity plays a significant role in the etiology of schizophrenic disorders. On the other hand, environmental factors apparently play a role too. As these researchers argue (Kety et al. 1971:304):

> Although this evidence does not support hypotheses that depend on the acquisition of schizophrenic behavior by learning from or imitation of other members of the family, it should be pointed out that our findings do not argue against the importance of environmental factors in the etiology of these disorders. Besides the presence in the household of an individual who exhibits some of the features of schizophrenia, there are many other aspects of life experience, including subtle personality characteristics, child rearing practices, nutritional habits, or even exposure to toxic or infectious agents, that may serve to evoke and elaborate one or another type of disorder in the schizophrenia spectrum in a genetically vulnerable individual.

Apparently, biogenetic studies of schizophrenia support an interactionist view: genetic and environmental factors *interact* to cause schizophrenic behaviors. As noted above, however, it is not yet established whether psychosocial or physical-chemical factors or *both* interact with genetic inheritance in causing schizophrenia. For example, Mosher et al. (1971) concluded from their study of twins discordant for schizophrenia (i.e., only one twin was schizophrenic) that many neurological abnormalities found in the schizophrenic twin could be caused by long-term treatment with tranquilizers or electroshock within the hospital. These authors leave the question open as to which environmental factors account for the differences in the discordant twins; they suggest, however, that different factors may be involved for different individuals.

Apparently, genes are normally *not* a decisive cause of schizophrenia; environmental factors also play a major role. It thus appears that we must think in terms of a genetic predisposition for schizophrenia. Some people may be predisposed to schizophrenic reactions, but environmental factors determine whether they manifest these behaviors. From twin studies and studies of high-risk populations (Mednick 1970) it also appears that the predisposition is not an all-or-nothing thing but rather a matter of degree. Some individuals are more predisposed than others, and, given equal environments, they are more likely to manifest schizophrenic symptoms. It is also possible that the German position is correct: some individuals are so predisposed that they will break down regardless of their environment; however, the evidence for this possibility remains inconclusive. Finally, while there is no unequivocal evidence that psychosocial factors play a role in the etiology of schizophrenia, there is no conclusive evidence that they do not. These questions must thus remain open.

Biological Causation

If genes play the role of predisposing factor, what is the role of biology? A person's biology is the result of the interaction between his genes and his environment. This is a fact frequently overlooked by specialists in the field. *Biology already contains environmental input.* Only a person's genes are strictly separable from environmental influence, and environment begins to influence an organism's biology upon conception. Intrauterine differences, for example, seem to account for the biological and behavioral differences found between genetically identical twins in infancy (Pollin 1965). Environmental influence begins in the womb, and differences in their womb environments produce differences in identical twins. An adult's biology, then, is the sum total of the interactions of his genotype and his environmental history. For example, persons who suffer from protein deficiency as children can suffer irreparable impairment in brain development. Such impairment will, of course, radically alter the way they interact with their environments, and this, in turn, will further alter their biology. A person's biology is thus only theoretically separable from his or her behavior; biology is both a cause and an effect of behavior. This is exactly the view supported by recent research on the other major psychoses, affective psychoses.

Biology and Mood Disorders

In an extremely provocative article, Akiskal and McKinney (1973) have attempted to synthesize the major behavioral, biological, and genetic theories of affective disorders. Affective disorders are disorders of mood; they include states of extreme elation and hyperactivity (mania) and states of depression. These authors present evidence that losing control over something extremely important in one's life (e.g., a loved one dies or rejects you) can reduce the amount of norepinephrine in the brain. This chemical normally facilitates the organism's ability to receive pleasure (rewards) through interaction with the environment. With the depletion of norepinephrine, the organism tends to withdraw and show no interest in the environment; these are the symptoms of depression. This syndrome has been produced experimentally in dogs and monkeys, and the same pattern has been observed clinically in humans.

Akiskal and McKinney propose that some individuals are more genetically predisposed to mood disorders than others. Approximately 10–15 percent of the population may, because of their genetic background, be highly susceptible to events precipitating depression. According to this theory, it is also possible for events in childhood to alter the "reward system" of the brain and render the person highly vulnerable to subsequent events. Depressions can be mild and transitory or they can be so severe that only somatic therapies (drugs, electroshock) are effective. To Akiskal and McKinney, this suggests two possibilities: (1) regardless of its cause, the disorder may assume biological proportions that are autonomous and therefore require somatic therapies; (2) severe depressions have an underlying genetic basis. Actually, these two possibilities are not necessarily mutually exclusive; either, or a mixture of both, could be present in any particular case.

Akiskal and McKinney thus reject a dichotomy between biology and environment. In their scheme, some persons may be more genetically predisposed than others, but experience can influence an individual's biology and further predispose him. In this regard, the authors point out that empirical evidence does *not* support the two-class taxonomy of depression, *reactive* and *endogenous*. As noted above, this dichotomy is officially accepted by both German and American psychiatry: endogenous depression springs from purely genetic causes, while reactive depression is a reaction to precipitating psychosocial events. When psychiatrists lack evidence for precipitating events, they diagnose endogenous depression. As Akiskal and McKinney point out, however, empirical studies have shown that the "lack" of such precipitating events is actually due to nonreporting (1973:21):

> The severely depressed patient is too disturbed to appraise fully the psychosocial context within which the illness manifests itself; upon clinical recovery, the frequency and type of stressful events, revealed by careful questioning, are no different from those in the "reactive" group. Depressive phenomena are neither inherently psychosocial nor biological. As a final common pathway, they are the culmination of processes that can be described in many frames of reference.

Apparently, diverse lines of evidence support an "interactionist" approach to the major psychoses. Schizophrenia and affective psychosis are both products of interactions between genetic makeup and environmental forces. Environment may act to precipitate or elaborate a psychosis in an extremely genetically vulnerable individual, or it may alter the biology of a less genetically predisposed individual and further predispose that individual to a particular type of breakdown. The role of psychosocial environmental variables is clearer in the etiology of depressive disorders than in schizophrenia. It has been empirically demonstrated that losing control over the environment not only can produce depression in a genetically vulnerable organism but can further predispose this organism to precipitating events in the future. Researchers have found it more difficult, however, to demonstrate such processes for schizophrenia. This is at least partially due to the fact that, compared to depression, it is more difficult to operationalize the concept of schizophrenia and then experimentally induce it in animals. So much of what is termed "schizophrenic" behavior depends on abnormal verbal behavior and on the breach of subtle social rules. These capacities are, of course, lacking in animals other than man. These difficulties notwithstanding, the fact that we lack conclusive evidence for psychosocial causes of schizophrenia does not mean that we can rule out such factors.

Are Mental Disorders Diseases?

The evidence presented above suggests that both genetic and environmental factors help cause schizophrenia and mood disorders. Does this mean that these conditions should be classified as "diseases"? This remains a moot point. Certainly, the mere fact that these conditions have biological correlates does not necessarily imply disease. *All* behavior has biological correlates. For example, some people are born with a greater genetic potential to become superb athletes. If raised in the proper environment, these people will develop biologies that allow them to perform extraordinary physical feats. Similarly, some people may be more predisposed to hallucinate than others. Raised in certain environments, their hallucinations might be termed "religious visions." In what sense are these hallucinations symptoms of a disease? Certainly, hallucinations are no more "genetic" or "biological" than athletic behavior—or than any other "normal" behavior. The discovery of biological correlates, then, does not necessarily qualify a condition as a disease.

Thomas Szasz (1960) has argued emphatically that these conditions do *not* technically qualify as diseases. Although the clinical universalists claim that psychosis is caused by a "neurological impairment," they have not been able to demonstrate this impairment empirically. Furthermore, even when biological correlates of psychotic states have been established, it is still not clear that these correlates should be considered an "impairment." This leads us to a consideration of the term "disease."

Sarbin (1969) has argued that "mental disorders" do not now meet the classic criteria for the definition of disease, namely, the presence of physical complaints by the patient and/or the presence of demonstrable organic pathology. The concept "organic pathology" implies organic abnormalities that inhibit the physiological processes that ultimately maintain life. Thus, an infected hangnail does not ordinarily threaten life; but it is clearly pathological, because it upsets processes that maintain bodily tissues, and, if it spreads, it can become life-threatening. No such pathology can now be demonstrated for the functional mental disorders; however, as some researchers point out, this does not preclude it from being demonstrated in the future.

Sarbin contends that the other criterion of disease, somatic complaints by the patient, is frequently not met in the case of mental disorders. Mental patients are not confined in mental hospitals because they have sore throats or because they complain of shortness of breath. Instead, complaints by others have been substituted for somatic complaints (Sarbin 1969:14). Mental patients are often confined because *other people have complained* about their *behavior*. Using this criterion, almost any behavior that is annoying to others can be defined as illness. For example, alcohol and drug use, which are associated with disruptive behavior, are now termed drug "abuse" or "addiction" and are officially classified as diseases. By this criterion, of course, smoking tobacco could also eventually be defined as "illness." Smoking is annoying to many, and it is certainly self-destructive.

Apparently, the specific biogenetic abnormalities that would definitely establish mental disorders as diseases (in the traditional sense of the term) have not been found. Nevertheless, it is useful to ask ourselves what type of evidence would establish this definition. First, researchers would have to show a clearly significant correlation between some biological trait and psychotic behavior. This trait would probably be a matter of deviation from a biological norm, just as fever represents a deviation from normal temperature. Second, researchers would have to establish a definite link between this trait and interference with life-maintenance processes. It is not enough to show that mental patients are biologically *different* (so are star athletes); one must also demonstrate that a particular trait constitutes or causes *organic pathology*. Only if these criteria were met would mental disorders be diseases in the traditional sense of the term.

Semantics or Profit?

The question whether mental disorders are diseases or not is not particularly fruitful. The criteria for any classification can always be expanded or delimited. Within the past few decades the criteria of disease have been expanded to include homosexuality, drug abuse, and alcoholism. Now the American Psychiatric Association has "declassified" homosexuality (Rosenhan 1975). Officially, then, homosexuality is no longer a disease, but it is still considered pathological by many clinicians. This illustrates the futility of discussing whether mental disorders are diseases. Practically anything can be classified officially as a disease if criteria are expanded to include it. The crucial question, then, is not whether a condition is a disease but, rather, what the advantages of such a classification are.

Szasz (1970) has argued that this classification has resulted in an enormous expansion of psychiatric power. Psychiatrists have become the final arbiters of what constitutes proper behavior in this society. They can decide which beliefs are rational and which behaviors are realistic. Thus, if a man believes that flying saucers are spying on the world, he is at best a crackpot and at worst a paranoid schizophrenic. On the other hand, if he believes that the acquisition of material goods should be life's primary goal or that the communists are trying to take over the world, he is considered not only "normal" but a "patriot." Szasz thus warns against the danger of allowing any one group to decide what is rational and what is not.

In Szasz's view, psychiatrists act as moral enforcers of a cultural belief system. They represent middle-class society's basic values, and they have the power to control those who deviate from these values. In this regard, Szasz (1970) has compared contemporary psychiatry to the Inquisition, which labeled deviant people "heretics" and "witches" in order to dispose of them. For Szasz, then, psychiatrists seldom operate as medical scientists. Rather, they represent the underlying values, standards, and beliefs of their society.

The data I presented in chapter 1 lend some support to

this view. Mental-health professionals in Germany and America were more like their publics than they were like each other in their basic conceptions of mental illness. This certainly would not have been the case had the questionnaire tested medical *information* about physical diseases rather than *opinions* about mental disorders. For example, if the questionnaire had asked for the symptoms of appendicitis or the anatomy of the heart, the medical personnel in the German and American staff samples would certainly have resembled each other more closely in their answers than they resembled their respective publics. As it was, in their basic underlying premises about the curability and causes of mental disorders, the two staff groups represented their own cultures' belief systems. In their premises they were Americans and Germans first and professionals second.

Some clinicians attempt to counter Szasz's attacks by asserting that the patient is the one who benefits most from the mental-illness model. According to this argument, patients are reassured by the physician when he diagnoses the illness and offers a prognosis and therapy (Kiev 1972:177; Siegler and Osmond 1974). This argument, of course, is not without merit. There *are* many mental patients who definitely believe they have profited from their entrance into the sick role and from the therapy they have received (Vonnegut 1974). On the other hand, this argument tends to ignore the following negative evidence: (1) the medical model does *not* allow mental patients to enter a conventional sick role; mental patients are socially stigmatized and frequently treated as prisoners; (2) lengthy hospitalization produces institutional syndrome; (3) attempts to shift to outpatient treatment, though partially successful, have resulted in increased recidivism rates; (4) the most common somatic therapies, antipsychotic drugs and electroshock, have never been subjected to long-term tests with adequate controls; consequently, they remain extremely controversial. Clinicians who support the medical approach to mental disorders must confront these points squarely. It is not enough merely to assert that "the biochemical causes will eventually be found" or that "the mentally ill profit from the medical approach." Regardless of the truth of these assertions, the problems listed above await solution, and practitioners who support the medical approach to mental disorders have an obligation to seek these solutions.

I have argued that biology is really inseparable from role behavior and that the tendency to dichotomize between biology and social roles has been a major impediment to communication and progressive research in this area. In the remainder of this chapter I will present a psychophysiological conception of "role" that allows evidence from both schools to be encompassed in one framework and so allows construction of a more parsimonious model.

The Psychophysiological Basis of Role

The clinical psychologist and role theorist T. R. Sarbin has posited a continuum (1954) of organismic involvement for role enactment (see Table 7). On the left of the spectrum is the "put-on" role, in which the person is consciously pretending and few of his organic processes are involved. As one moves along the continuum from left to right, the physiological involvement of the organism increases: more biological systems are mobilized, and the role becomes less consciously voluntary. For example, stage 2, Ritual Acting, is consciously voluntary, and the stage actor's physiological responses do not necessarily match the role being enacted. In stage 3, Engrossed (Method) Acting, the stage actor loses awareness that he is acting, and his physiological responses are appropriate to the role he plays. In a word, the method actor does not *play* Hamlet, he *becomes* Hamlet.

Normal, everyday roles lie along stages 1–4. In everyday life we are, in a sense, "method actors" most of the time. The roles we enact (doctor-patient, mother-son, teacher-student), are not generally accessible to our own analysis and scrutiny, and these roles do effectively mobilize appropriate physiological reactions. In comparing the stage actor to the man in the street, Goffman (1959:73) points out that neither has very adequate "stage directions." Neither has been coached in the thousands of subtleties that make up even a five-minute role enactment, e.g., subtle eye movements, the relative tension of various muscle groups, postures, intonation, inflection, and kinetics. Neither the stage

TABLE 7   Continuum of Organismic Involvement in Social Roles

```
                                           7. Voodoo
                                              Death
                                      _____
                                   6. States
                                      of Pos-
                                      session
                               _____
                            5. His-
                               trionic
                               Neu-
                               rosis
                        _____
                     4. Classi-
                        cal Hyp-
                        notic
                        Role-
                        Taking
                 _____
              3. En-
                 grossed
                 Acting
          _____
       2. Ritual
          Acting
    _____
 1. Casual
    Role En-
    actment
_____
Zero.
Noninvolve-
ment
```

0	1	2	3	4	5	6	7	8
Role and Self Differentiated: Minimal Organic Involvement						Role and Self Undifferentiated: Maximum Organic Involvement		

Adapted from Sarbin and Allen (1968:493). This conception of social role allows a reconciliation of the biomedical and the social-role approaches to mental disorders. In the model proposed in the text, certain, "insane" behaviors are initially "put on" and thus would begin at stage 1, above. As these behaviors are reinforced by the social environment, they tend to become internalized and thus are no longer differentiated from the self and its organic systems (stages 3–7). This process of internalization is fundamental to virtually all theories of mental disorders as social roles. In contrast, other behaviors begin as "spontaneous" psychophysiological alterations that involve the entire organism, e.g., acute schizophrenia or depres-

actor nor the layman can formulate in advance all the subtleties that he will utilize to play his scene. But, as Goffman
(1959:73) notes, "the incapacity of the ordinary individual
to formulate in advance the movements of his eyes and
body does not mean that he will not express himself through
these devices in a way that is dramatized and pre-formed in
his repertoire of actions. In short, we all act better than we
know how."

Somewhere between stage 4 (Hypnotic Role-Taking) and
stage 5 (Hysteria) in Table 7 would lie the psychophysiological basis for psychosomatic disorders: behaviors learned in
particular social milieus that produce demonstrable organic
pathology. On the right end of the continuum is Voodoo
Death, in which the role expectations of the hexed man are
so powerful, and his organismic involvement is so great,
that he may ultimately go into shock and die (Cannon 1942).

In this scheme, then, biology is seen as inseparable from
social roles in any but the most consciously put-on, voluntary behaviors. In the following pages I will attempt to
demonstrate that this conception of "role" allows the
biomedical and social-role perspectives both to be encompassed in one framework. In this discussion I will not compare the phenomena of mental disorders with the different
behaviors listed on the continuum in Table 7. Those behaviors were used merely to illustrate degrees of physiological
involvement in culturally patterned behavior (Sarbin and
Allen 1968). Consequently, relating these specific behaviors to mental disorders, while potentially valuable, is not
really crucial to our discussion. Instead, I will demonstrate
how this psychophysiological conception of role illuminates
discrepancies between various social-role theories and between them and the biomedical approach.

To explain how this conception of role can encompass
the various states termed "mental disorders" in our cul-

sion. As these behaviors come under environmental influence, however, they may
be precipitated by environmental events and can become habitual in this respect.
In this sense, they also become something of a *conditioned response*. The
symptomatology of a chronic mental patient probably includes a mixture of
behaviors, some of which were "learned" but now mobilize organic systems,
and some of which began as "organic" reactions but now are "conditioned responses."

ture, I would like to draw on Albert Cain's excellent article (1964) on "playing crazy" in borderline children. Cain presents cogent clinical evidence for the following propositions: (1) Institutionalized children learn to play at being crazy. They make frequent reference to this fact and even threaten to "act crazy" in the future in order to get their own way. (2) The images of madness used by the children are constructed from popular stereotypes and conceptions. (3) The children are frequently rewarded for adopting "crazy" symptoms. Their threats and tantrums may earn them respect, and their "odd role" grants them a personal and social license not unlike that enjoyed by the "town character." (4) Even when the child is slipping toward or is virtually in a psychotic state, he may pretend in a frenzied fashion to be crazy. Or, as Cain (1964:284) puts it, he pretends to be crazier than he is at the moment.

Now there seem to be three different phenomena embodied in these four propositions. First, the individual may learn to "act" crazy. This acting may at first involve a conscious pretense; at times the children are very obviously pretending and readily admit this. This role enactment would lie somewhere between zero and stage 1 on our continuum. Alternatively, the individual may learn to act crazy but may do so less consciously, e.g., one child may unwittingly imitate or model his behavior on the other children's. This process would fall somewhere between stages 1 and 4.

The second phenomenon in Cain's description involves what the social-role theorists would call "role internalization" or "incorporation." As the child begins to act crazy, the inadvertent reinforcement these behaviors receive from the environment (within or without the hospital) may cause them to be internalized. That is to say, organismic involvement increases, and the behaviors become less consciously voluntary. Thus, although these behaviors may begin at zero or stage 1 on the continuum, they gradually, through the reinforcement they receive, move into more involved and less voluntary stages. Some aspect of this scheme underlies (implicitly) all theories of mental illness as social roles. But authors do vary in their emphasis. As we saw above, Braginsky et al. stress the fact that some patients are consciously pretending or, at the very least, are producing, whenever the necessity arises, symptomatic behaviors to manipulate the staff (1969:171–72):

> It is obvious that rational goal-directed behavior does not guarantee that the individual appreciates what he is up to. It is equally obvious that the residents described in this book frequently must have been consciously manipulative; many of our findings would be inexplicable without making such an assumption. All we are claiming is that it is not necessary to suppose that the choice to become a mental patient always reflects a state of conscious volition.

In contrast to the Braginskys, Goffman (1961:149) and Scheff (1966:88) would, according to our scheme, emphasize the process of internalization that moves the behaviors from stage 1 to more involved stages: symptoms may begin as conscious pretense or unconscious imitation, but reinforcement from laymen and staff causes these behaviors to become involuntary and habitual.

The third state is the psychotic state to which Cain refers. Cain never tells us how this state differs from the other two, but he himself implicitly differentiates it from the other two, and evidently the children do also. Presumably, such states involve psychophysiological alterations that result in the classic symptoms of psychosis: cognitive disturbances, social withdrawal, and disturbed affect. Such alterations are used to support biomedical theories of mental illness. These psychophysiological alterations lead to markedly bizarre behavior in some individuals, and, as proposed above, it is presumably such cases that best support the clinical-universalist argument. The question now arises as to how social learning and role expectations may affect these "acute psychotic states." The preceding two types of "mad" behavior discussed by Cain clearly involve role internalization, and even outspoken critics of the social-role approach admit that long-term hospitalization has produced chronic deviant roles of this type (Murphy 1976; Gove 1975a, 1975b; Chauncey 1975). However, these same critics argue (either explicitly or implicitly) that psychotic states are independent of role expectations and indeed are really quite separate and distinct from the "secondary deviance" produced by institutions (Rosenbaum 1969; Murphy 1976; Chauncy 1975:249). This type of argument perpetuates the hoary nature-nurture dichotomy and tends to confuse the issues. I propose to demonstrate that social learning is important in molding all symptoms of mental disorders but that it affects symptoms differently at different stages of a patient's career.

As we have seen, careful studies of hereditary factors support an interactional approach to mental disorders. Genes and environment, including psychosocial factors, apparently interact to produce mental disorders. It is quite plausible, however, that the role of social learning in structuring symptoms is different at different stages of a patient's career. The evidence for this proposition is as follows. Extensive clinical evidence suggests that social learning helps to determine the timing and content of symptoms. Bowers (1974), for example, uses clinical data to marshal an impressive case for this thesis. He proposes that traumatic experiences structure the symptoms of emerging psychosis in two ways: they act as precipitating factors, and they emerge in the content of the symptoms. Bowers thus proposes that the initial symptoms of psychosis possess a structure but that this structure, like the structure of dreams, is somewhat idiosyncratic and abstruse. For example, the loss of a loved one might precipitate a depressed state in which the patient suffered from the delusions that everyone hated him and that he was being punished for some imagined sin. This proposition, that social experience affects the content of symptoms, is generally accepted by even the staunchest defenders of the clinical approach (Meehl 1962; Forster 1962).

Given that social learning molds the content and timing of initial symptoms, we must ask whether this constitutes a social role. The florid, most acute symptoms of emerging psychosis as described by Bowers probably least resemble what is normally considered a social role. Although social learning has helped structure these symptoms, it has not done so in a way that is comprehensible to other members of the culture. Perhaps an expert on emerging psychosis will divine a structure and be able to predict the patient's behavior within certain limits, but the average layman will not. Indeed, it is precisely because the behavior *is* incomprehensible in terms of normal role expectations that it is considered crazy. Generally speaking, when a culturally acceptable motive for a behavior can be found, the act will be considered sane (Jaeckel and Wieser 1970; Edgerton 1966, 1969). Given these considerations, the concept "social role" is probably least fruitful in analyzing this part of the patient's career.

During and after the process of being identified and labeled mentally ill, however, the individual is increasingly subjected to significant others' expectations concerning mental illness. The expectations become most systematic and formal when the patient is hospitalized. The staff, having divorced the patient from normal roles and supports, expects the patient to act out their version of "mental patient," and, of course, the staff is empowered to reward the behaviors it desires and to punish those it does not. Presumably, then, the treatment phase, and particularly hospitalization, most favors the production of a recognizable, deviant social role. This proposition is consistent with the evidence examined in the preceding chapters.

At the end of chapter 2 we saw that, initially, significant others tend to deny the existence of symptoms. The prepatient must repeatedly breach others' expectations before they begin to define his acts as symptoms of mental illness. I argued that this denial arose in part because the symptoms did not match popular stereotypes and because laymen, whether German or American, had no systematic expectations concerning mental illness. Thus, it is difficult to see how cultural conceptions of mental illness could effectively mold a *role* of mental illness at this point. In contrast, in chapter 2 my data showed that hospitalized German and American mental patients tended to utilize coping tactics that were predictable from their own culture's (and staff's) conceptions of mental illness. Moreover, in chapters 3 and 4 we saw that long-term hospitalization does produce an "institutional syndrome" that resembles psychotic symptoms and that frequently results in continued hospitalization. Apparently, then, several lines of evidence support this proposition: "social learning," as a conceptual tool, may be extremely important in understanding all phases of a patient's career, but it is the treatment phase that more effectively produces predictable and recognizable deviant social roles.

In the proposed scheme, then, social experience not only helps determine the onset, timing, and content of symptoms; it also can continue to structure symptomatology throughout a patient's career (as Bleuler [1950] proposed). For example, after the first psychotic episode, the subject's threshold for entering this "altered state of consciousness" might be lowered. Anxiety could provoke another episode, and the person's fear of this possibility and his uncertainty about his sanity might become part of a self-fulfilling prophecy. The more the patient feared slipping into one of these states, the more he would become likely to do so. If we assume that these states can be precipitated by environmental events, it is quite possible that they could become habitual in this respect. That is to say, they too could become something of a conditioned response. If this is true, then, in a disorder of long standing, it would be difficult if not impossible to distinguish among these three different classes of behaviors: (1) behaviors that began as consciously "put-on" mad roles but became internalized; (2) behaviors that began during acute psychotic states as idiosyncratic expressions but came to be mediated by the environment and could be habitually triggered by specific events; (3) behaviors that emerged as specific responses to institutional life. The symptomatology of a chronic mental patient probably includes a mixture of all these behaviors, which might ultimately become indistinguishable clinically, phenomenologically, and perhaps even biochemically.

Conclusion

The model of psychosis presented in this chapter is admittedly speculative and impressionistic. Ultimate verification or rejection awaits further research. There are, of course, many aspects of psychosis that this model cannot presently explain, and, no doubt, a comprehensive model of psychosis will ultimately involve a multiplicity of genetic, physiological, psychological, and sociological factors. For the present, however, the model presented here, though speculative and imprecise, does seem able to encompass a broad spectrum of evidence from a variety of approaches.

If even partially correct, the argument set forth in this book has the following implications. First, mental hospitals, as they presently exist, should be abolished. Like our prisons, they are counterproductive. Both tend to perpetuate what they are supposed to eliminate: chronic social deviants. England has already embarked on a program to eliminate mental hospitals within twenty-five years. America is beginning to do the same. For those with deep-seated psychological disturbances, therapeutic communities should be created along the lines suggested by Thomas Lambo (1964), the Nigerian psychiatrist who has acted as assistant director general of the World Health Organization in Geneva. In his scheme, mental patients are not separated from society. A family member accompanies a patient to the therapeutic community and remains involved in his treatment. Various types of agencies are involved, including psychiatric, legal, and religious. For those with transitory behavioral problems, crisis counseling centers should include psychological counseling, legal aid, and social-welfare counseling and aid. Several states have begun to establish such programs, and some counties have for several years avoided state hospitalization of their patients. Patients are treated instead in community clinics, day-care centers, and halfway houses (Gottesfeld 1976). These improvements notwithstanding, the problem is not nearly solved. In many cases, discharging patients has merely resulted in a revolving-door policy. The average length of time in the hospital has decreased, but readmission rates have risen commensurately (National Institute of Mental Health 1971). For the people who are "not important to anybody," there is still no place to go (Feldman 1974; Talbott 1974; Aviram and Segal 1973).

Second, both mental-health professionals and the general public should become more aware of the powerful effect of expectations. If teachers' expectations in the classroom can produce brighter or duller students (Rosenthal and Jacobsen 1968), and experimenters' expectations can produce their own reality (Orne 1962), then the hospital staff's expectations about mental patients can have similar effects.

If, relative to Germans, the American staff and public believe that the mentally ill look and act in bizarre ways, then it is probable that their expectations will be rewarded. Certainly, my observations on German and American wards tend to support this notion.

Third, Americans should carefully reexamine their attitudes toward individual effort and social welfare. As my research suggests, the problem of patient chronicity does not lend itself to simplistic analyses of "free will versus determinism." Patients do have to "try to get better," but whether they do so or not depends to a great extent on how they are treated by the staff and what they have waiting for them on the outside. Experiments in behavior modification have proved that an effective way of getting patients out of the hospital and keeping them out is to provide them with positive rewards for staying out. This reward may at first consist of something as simple as ice cream, but ultimately it must consist of creating superior options in the outside world. This means better jobs, better living conditions, and help in constructing more meaningful interpersonal relations. The assumption that people are responsible for their fate through lack of will and personal effort is simplistic. It is also misleading to assume that a purely biomedical approach is adequate. Only by rejecting these assumptions have communities begun to construct programs that minimize institutionalization and recidivism.

Finally, we need more research on the causes and cures of mental disorders. A proper research strategy would include a multiplicity of parameters: genetic, physiological, developmental, and cultural. The present study suggests that only by thus recognizing the complexity of human behaviors can we finally begin to solve the problems of mental disorders.

Appendix

**TABLE A   Demographic Characteristics of German Student Sample
(N = 552) and American Student Sample (N = 728)**

Characteristic	Percentage of German Students	Percentage of American Students
Sex:		
Male	53.0	51.0
Female	47.0	49.0
Age:		
14–15	11.1	20.0
16–17	59.6	52.0
18–19	25.4	22.0
20–22	3.8	6.0
Ethnic group:		
Chicano	—	0.7
Black	—	0.6
White	98.6	0.6
Indian	—	1.9
Foreign student	1.3	0.2
Asian American	—	1.0
Other	—	1.9
Approximate family income:		
Under $2,000	n. a.*	2.6
$2,000–$5,600	n. a.	12.7
$5,600–$7,000	n. a.	5.9
$7,000–$11,800	n. a.	25.8
$11,800–$17,000	n. a.	30.4

TABLE A (continued)

Characteristic	Percentage of German Students	Percentage of American Students
$17,000–$20,000	n. a.	10.1
Over $20,000	n. a.	12.5
Marital status:		
Married	n. a.	3.0
Single	n. a.	97.0
Religion:		
Protestant	56.8	30.4
Catholic	35.3	25.9
Jewish	0.2	0.6
Agnostic	—	5.6
No preference	1.8	14.9
Other	5.9	22.5
Occupation (of father or principal earner):		
Laborer (manual)	25.4	35.2
White-collar employee	31.2	26.5
Civic official (*Beamte*), or licensed professional	11.4	18.1
Entrepreneur	20.7	5.4
Farmer	0.2	1.4
Retired	0.7	1.4
Unemployed	—	4.4
Unknown	10.1	7.6

*n.a. = not available.

TABLE B   Demographic Characteristics of German Mental-Hospital Staff Sample (N = 102)

Characteristic	Percentage	Characteristic	Percentage
Sex:		Medical administrator	4.9
Male	71.8	Social worker	2.9
Female	28.2	Psychologist	1.9
Age:		Therapist	1.9
15–20	1.9	Attendant (male)	8.7
21–30	33.0	Nurse	13.6
31–40	40.8	*Length of service in*	
41–50	18.4	*mental hospitals*:	
51–60	5.8	0–3 months	15.5
Marital status:		4–6 months	5.8
Single	35.9	7 months–2 years	23.3
Married	56.3	3–5 years	22.3
Divorced	6.8	6–10 years	15.5
Widowed	1.0	11–20 years	15.5
Years of education:		Over 20 years	1.9
6–8 (Volkschule)	1.9	*Hospital*:	
9–11 (Mittelschule)	2.9	Bremen Municipal	
12–15 (Oberschule,		Psychiatric Clinic	21.1
Fachschule,		Hannover University	
or Berufschule)	20.3	Psychiatric Clinic	16.7
17–20 (Hochschule)	74.8	Düsseldorf State	
Present position:		Mental Hospital	24.4
Intern	7.8	Frankfurt University	
Resident	31.1	Psychiatric Clinic	36.7
Psychiatrist	27.2	Köppern State	
		Mental Hospital	

TABLE C   American Mental-Hospital Staff Sample ($N = 79$)

Characteristic	Percentage	Characteristic	Percentage
Sex:		*Length of service in*	
Male	66.2	*mental hospitals:*	
Female	33.7	0–3 months	6.3
Age:		4–6 months	5.0
15–20	1.2	7 months–2 years	22.5
21–25	6.3	3–5 years	13.7
26–30	17.5	6–10 years	18.8
31–35	12.5	11–20 years	23.7
36–40	7.5	Over 20 years	10.0
41–50	26.2	*Position:*	
51–60	20.0	Psychiatric	
Over 60	8.7	Technician	25.0
Years of education:		Nurse	3.7
12–13	17.5	Psychiatrist	37.5
14–15	12.5	Resident	22.5
16–17	5.0	Intern	3.7
18–19	5.0	M.D. administration	1.3
20–21	45.0	Social worker	2.5
Over 21	15.0	Psychologist	1.2
Marital status:		Student aide	2.5
Single	8.7	*Type of hospital:*	
Married	75.0	State Mental	
Divorced	11.0	Hospital	68.7
Separated	1.2	University	21.2
Widowed	2.5	General	
Religion:		(psychiatric ward)	1.3
Protestant	45.0	Veteran's	
Catholic	17.5	Administration	6.2
Jewish	6.3	Combinations	
Latter Day Saints	13.7	of above	2.5
No preference	13.7		
Other	2.5		
Unknown	1.2		

TABLE D   **Demographic Characteristics for German Patient Sample
(N = 112) and American Patient
Sample (N = 110)**

Characteristic	Percentage of German Patients	Percentage of American Patients
Sex:		
Male	45.5	41.8
Female	54.5	58.2
Marital status:		
Married	29.5	18.2
Single	46.4	42.7
Divorced	11.6	24.5
Separated	—	10.9
Widowed	12.5	3.6
Ethnic group:		
Black	—	11.8
White	100.0	80.9
Chicano	—	7.3
Age:		
15–19	1.8	0.9
20–29	13.4	32.7
30–39	10.7	22.7
40–49	19.6	19.1
50–59	21.4	16.4
60–69	25.9	7.3
Over 70	7.1	0.9
Type of commitment:		
Voluntary	23.2	60.0
Involuntary	76.8	19.1
Admission initially voluntary, changed to involuntary	—	—

TABLE D (continued)

Characteristic	Percentage of German Patients	Percentage of American Patients
Diagnosis:		
Schizophrenic	34.8	70.0
Affective disorder	26.8	5.5
Neurotic	5.4	12.7
Alcoholic	14.3	1.8
Drug abuse	2.7	2.7
Senile psychosis	5.4	0.9
Organic psychosis	2.7	3.6
Chronic brain syndrome	—	2.7
Epilepsy	4.5	—
Other	3.6	—
History of confinements:		
First stay in hospital	36.6	31.8
In target hospital before	6.3	29.1
In other hospitals before	57.2	39.1
Total Time in Mental Hospitals:		
0–3 months	25.0	38.2
4–6 months	9.8	6.4
7 months–2 years	29.5	14.5
2–5 years	13.4	17.3
5–10 years	8.0	10.9
10–20 years	12.5	5.5
Over 20 years	1.8	7.3

Figures are for all patients who completed any one part of the study, e.g., the semantic differentials. Not all patients completed all parts of the patient interview due to transfers, releases, and patient "interviewability." Substitutions were randomly selected from the patient population.

126   Appendix

TABLE E   The Sixty-Item "Conceptions of Mental Illness"
          Questionnaire, with Means and Standard Deviations

INSTRUCTIONS

You are being asked to participate in a study of mental health problems. Your participation will supply valuable information to those responsible for the nation's health.

On the following pages you will find a number of statements about health problems. We want to know how much you agree or disagree with each of the statements. To the right of each statement you can find a rating scale:

Disagree   Agree
  1   2   3   4   5   6   7

[ ][ ][ ][ ][ ][ ][ ]

The points along the scale (1,2,3, ... 7) can be interpreted as follows:

1. Completely disagree
2. Mostly disagree
3. Disagree more than agree
4. Neutral
5. Agree more than disagree
6. Mostly agree
7. Completely agree

The use of the scale can be illustrated with the following statement:

"Smoking causes lung cancer."

If you agreed completely with this statement, you would place a mark in column 7. If you agreed slightly with the statement, you would place a mark in column 5. If you mostly disagreed with the statement, you would place a mark in column 2. In this manner you can indicate the extent to which you agree or disagree with each of the statements on the following pages.

Like everyone else, you will probably feel that you do not know the answer to some of the statements. When this occurs please make the best guess that you can.

Please make your marks inside the agreement and disagreement boxes of the scales. Do it like this:

Disagree   Agree
  1   2   3   4   5   6   7

[ ][ ][ ][ ][ ][X][ ]

Do *not* do it like this:

```
        Disagree                        Agree
         1     2     3     4     5     6     7
       ┌─────┬─────┬─────┬─────┬─────┬─────┬─────┐
       │     │     │     │     │    ✗│     │     │
       └─────┴─────┴─────┴─────┴─────┴─────┴─────┘
```

Please make sure that you make a mark for each statement. Leave none of the statements blank and make only one mark for each. You should not spend more than a few seconds marking each statement. If it is difficult for you to make up your mind, make the best guess that you can and go on to the next one.

	GS*	GStu	AS	AStu	SD
1. The mentally ill pay little attention to their personal appearance.	3.9	3.9	4.0	3.7	1.7
2. People who keep themselves occupied with pleasant thoughts seldom become mentally ill.	1.5	2.6	2.9	2.9	1.7
3. Few people who enter mental hospitals ever leave.	1.7	3.0	1.9	2.6	1.7
4. Older people have fewer emotional problems than younger people.	2.6	2.7	2.3	2.9	1.8
5. People cannot maintain good mental health without the support of strong persons in their environment.	2.6	3.1	3.3	4.2	2.0
6. Will power alone will not cure mental disorders.	6.2	4.9	5.6	4.7	1.8
7. Women have no more emotional problems than men do.	5.0	4.0	4.2	4.0	2.0
8. X-rays of the head will not tell whether a person is likely to become insane.	5.8	4.6	6.2	5.4	1.9
9. Emotional problems do little damage to the individual.	1.7	1.5	2.1	1.8	1.2

---

*AStu = American high school students ($N = 728$). GStu = German high-school students (555). AS = American mental-hospital staff ($N = 79$). GS = German mental-hospital staff (102). SD = standard deviation. A mean of 7 signifies total agreement; a mean of 1, total disagreement; a mean of 4, neutrality. See text for description of samples and instrument.

TABLE E (continued)	GS	GStu	AS	AStu	SD
10. Psychiatrists try to teach mental patients to hold in their strong emotions.	3.5	4.0	2.4	2.9	2.0
11. Mental illness can usually be helped by a vacation or change of scene.	1.5	2.1	3.0	3.6	1.7
12. Disappointments affect children as much as they do adults.	4.5	5.0	5.6	5.0	2.1
13. The main job of the psychiatrist is to recommend hobbies and other ways for the mental patient to occupy his mind.	2.5	3.8	2.2	3.4	2.0
14. The insane laugh more than normal people.	1.8	3.2	2.3	2.8	1.7
15. Psychiatrists try to show the mental patient where his ideas are incorrect.	3.8	4.6	4.5	4.3	1.8
16. Mental disorder is not a hopeless condition.	5.5	5.5	6.4	6.0	1.7
17. Mental health is one of the most important national problems.	5.2	4.9	6.0	5.5	1.7
18. Mental disorder is usually brought on by physical causes.	2.7	2.8	2.6	3.3	1.6
19. It is easier for women to get over emotional problems than it is for men.	2.2	2.6	2.7	3.3	1.7
20. A change of climate seldom helps an emotional disorder.	5.4	4.6	4.9	4.0	1.7
21. The best way to mental health is by avoiding morbid thoughts.	1.8	3.1	3.2	3.4	1.9
22. There is not much that can be done for a person who develops a mental disorder.	2.0	1.8	1.6	2.0	1.4
23. Mental disorder is one of the most damaging illnesses that a a person can have.	5.2	5.4	4.8	4.6	1.9
24. Children sometimes have mental breakdowns as severe as those of adults.	5.0	5.2	6.5	5.2	1.8
25. Nervous breakdowns seldom have a physical origin.	4.3	4.6	4.1	3.6	1.9
26. Most of the people in mental hospitals speak in words that can be understood.	5.3	4.6	5.8	4.8	1.7
27. Mental health is largely a matter of trying hard to control the emotions.	2.4	3.0	3.1	3.9	1.8

TABLE E (continued)	GS	GStu	AS	AStu	SD
28. If a person concentrates on happy memories, he will not be bothered by unpleasant things in the present.	2.6	3.1	2.7	2.8	1.8
29. The mentally ill have not received enough guidance from the important people in their lives.	2.7	3.4	4.2	4.0	1.8
30. Women are as emotionally healthy as men.	5.8	5.6	5.7	5.0	1.8
31. The seriousness of the mental-health problem in this country has been exaggerated.	2.3	2.2	2.3	2.7	1.5
32. Helping the mentally ill person with his financial and social problems often improves his condition.	4.5	3.1	5.6	4.7	1.8
33. Mental patients usually make a good adjustment to society when they are released.	3.1	3.9	4.1	4.1	1.5
34. The good psychiatrist acts like a father to his patients.	4.0	5.1	3.2	4.1	1.8
35. Early adulthood is more of a danger period for mental illness than later years.	3.5	3.3	4.3	4.5	1.6
36. Almost any disease that attacks the nervous system is likely to bring on insanity.	1.6	3.1	2.5	3.2	1.7
37. You can tell a person who is mentally ill from his appearance.	2.5	3.0	2.8	2.7	1.8
38. People who become mentally ill have little will power.	1.8	3.0	2.9	3.5	1.7
39. Women are more likely to develop mental disorders than men.	2.0	2.6	3.0	3.4	1.6
40. Most mental disturbances in adults can be traced to emotional experiences in childhood.	3.2	4.3	5.2	4.9	1.7
41. People who have little sexual desire are more likely to have a "nervous breakdown" than are other people.	2.2	3.0	2.8	3.2	1.7
42. A person can avoid worry by keeping busy.	3.1	3.2	4.1	3.8	2.0
43. A poor diet often leads to feeble-mindedness.	1.6	2.8	2.8	3.7	1.7

TABLE E (continued)	GS	GStu	AS	AStu	SD
44. Emotionally upset persons are often found in important positions in business.	3.2	3.4	4.5	4.4	1.6
45. Good emotional habits can be taught to children in school as easily as spelling can.	2.0	3.2	3.6	4.1	1.9
46. The eyes of the insane are glassy.	1.7	2.8	1.9	2.9	1.6
47. When a person is recovering from a mental illness, it is best not to discuss the treatment that he has had.	3.1	4.5	2.6	3.9	1.9
48. People who go from doctor to doctor with many complaints know that there is nothing really wrong with them.	2.4	3.6	2.3	3.5	1.9
49. A person cannot rid himself of unpleasant memories by trying hard to forget them.	5.2	5.6	4.7	4.8	1.8
50. The main job of the psychiatrist is to explain to the patient the origin of his troubles.	4.1	5.3	3.7	4.6	1.8
51. Most suicides occur because of rejection in love.	3.5	3.8	3.5	4.5	1.9
52. People who are likely to have a nervous breakdown pay little attention to their personal appearance.	2.4	2.9	3.6	3.3	2.7
53. Most of the time psychiatrists have difficulty in telling whether or not a patient's mental disorder is curable.	3.7	4.0	4.1	3.9	1.5
54. Children usually do not forget about frightening experiences in a short time.	4.7	5.3	5.2	5.2	1.8
55. Books on "peace of mind" prevent many people from developing nervous breakdowns.	2.0	2.5	3.3	3.3	1.5
56. Most clergymen will encourage a person with a mental disorder to see a psychiatrist.	4.2	4.5	4.8	4.5	1.8
57. Physical exhaustion does not lead to a nervous breakdown.	4.1	4.1	3.9	3.5	2.0
58. The adult who needs a great deal of affection is likely to have had little affection in childhood.	3.8	5.0	4.7	4.9	1.9

TABLE E (continued)	GS	GStu	AS	AStu	SD
59. Physical rest will not prevent a mental disorder.	5.6	4.8	4.9	4.5	1.7
60. Most of the people who seek psychiatric help need the treatment.	5.4	4.3	5.7	4.2	1.8

Now that you have completed the questionnaire would you please check to make sure that you have done the following things:

1. Rated your agreement or disagreement with every statement in the questionnaire. If you have failed to mark a single statement, we will be unable to use your questionnaire.
2. Made only one mark for each statement.

THANK YOU AGAIN FOR YOUR HELP IN THIS RESEARCH.

Notes

Introduction

1. The concepts "mental illness" and "social role" will be defined and discussed more fully in chapter 5. In the meantime, the terms mental "illness," "insanity," "disorders," and "disease" will be used interchangeably. "Social role" refers to culturally conditioned behavior patterns that can also mobilize physiological responses (see Sarbin and Allen 1968). Throughout the book I tend to equate "universalism" with the medical approach to mental disorders. It is, of course, possible that a person could argue for the universality of symptoms and not support the medical approach to diagnosis and treatment. Some behavioral psychologists might fit in this category. In practice, however, I believe that most universalists support the psychiatric perspective (e.g., Murphy 1976; Gove 1975b; Kiev 1972; Meehl 1962; Kety 1974; Chauncey 1975; Forster 1962; Margetts and Leighton in Ciba Foundation Symposium 1965:23–24).

2. In presenting the results of this study, it is assumed that there is considerable overlap between the two nationalities. Frequently the German and American groups differed significantly on a question, but inspection showed a majority of both groups had responded similarly to it. This type of overlap is to be expected, given the cultural similarities between the two countries. American culture stems from northern European roots; English is a Germanic language; and both countries are capitalistic and highly industrialized. These cultural similarities limit the number of variables and thus make the differences which did emerge more meaningful.

Chapter 1

1. The American student sample does lack ethnic and religious diversity (see Appendix, Table A), and in this sense it is not representative of American populations. It was reasoned, however, that inclusion of ethnic and religious minorities could introduce the possibility of subcultural traits acting as confounding variables. Moreover, insofar as the majority of the American students were white and Christian, they were representative of what has traditionally been described as the dominant ethos of the United States. It was for these reasons that school districts containing large concentrations of ethnic and religious minorities were not included in the sample.

2. This is probably not a serious bias because the German university hospital that provided most of the physicians (Frankfurt am Main) functioned as a municipal clinic and therefore more closely resembled nonuniversity facilities in the

American sample than it would resemble the prototype university clinic. The age bias, though slight, could be important. However, as represented by older physicians, traditional German psychiatry is almost exclusively biologically oriented. Consequently, any bias resulting from the greater number of young physicians in the German sample should serve only to *decrease* the inter-cultural differences that were found. Similarly, it is also quite probable that the "volunteer bias" tended to select for more avant-garde or progressive physicians in both countries. More conservative physicians tend to be skeptical of such research and, in the experience of this writer, are less likely to cooperate. In any event, there is no reason to suppose that volunteer bias would operate differently among mental-health professionals in the two countries.

3. During the translation of the questionnaire, it was discovered that many of the expected conceptual differences were encoded in terminological differences. For example, the term "mental illness" is probably best translated by *psychisch-krank*, but this term is definitely not a part of the middle-class vernacular. The common German word *geisteskrank* is more akin to our word "insane," with its concomitant legal connotations. German psychiatrists also generally interpret the word *geisteskrank* as implying schizophrenia (endogenous and virtually incurable in their view). This means that the word *geisteskrank* is commonly used where we would use "insane" or "psychotic"; but it is also used where we might employ the more euphemistic "mentally ill," and the inadequacy of *geisteskrank* as a translation reflects the conceptual differences the statements were designed to study.

Chapter 2

1. A few patients with "organic" conditions appear in the samples. This is ex-plained by the fact that, when choosing interviewees, we accepted the ward physician's assurance that a particular patient's confinement was due to func-tional disorders. In a few cases the ward psychiatrist's evaluation differed from the "official" diagnosis, which appeared in the patient's record. It is the "official" diagnosis, taken from the patient's record, which appears, along with the other demographic variables, in the Appendix (Table D).

2. As detailed in chapter 4, cross-national studies indicate that "schizophrenia" may encompass a much broader field of behavior in America than in other nations. Gurland et al. (1969) and Kendell et al. (1971) found that American psychiatrists tend to diagnose certain patients as schizophrenic who would be diagnosed by British psychiatrists as "affectively ill," "neurotic," or suffering from "personality disorders." The differences between German and American diagnoses depicted in the Appendix (Table D) generally approximate the dif-ferences found between British and American classifications (Cooper et al. 1969). If we can assume that German psychiatrists would diagnose a subgroup of the American schizophrenic group more or less as the British did, the dis-crepancies between the patient samples disappear.

3. The results of the Twenty Statements Test presented a problem for analysis. German patients were much more inclined than Americans to complete all of the twenty statements. German patients ($N = 79$) left 650 statements blank, whereas the Americans ($N = 84$) left 1,264. Because the tendency of the Ger-man patients to answer was greater than the Americans', there was a greater

probability that a German patient would land in any category. In an attempt to control for this tendency, patient responses were analyzed in terms of percentages. If one of an American patient's four responses referred to his physical state, he was coded as having 25 percent of his responses in that category.

Unfortunately, this procedure does not control for zero responses. Americans having generally fewer responses would have a greater tendency to have zero responses on any category than the Germans. Thus, any cultural difference which arises from a greater number of Americans giving zero responses might reflect merely the Germans' greater tendency to answer rather than the Germans' greater tendency to characterize themselves in terms of a specific category. The Germans' greater tendency to answer might thus explain the differences in the categories "Health: Unspecific References" and "Status and Role," but this tendency *cannot* explain the cultural differences found in the categories "Physical," "Allusions to Patient Role," and "Inappropriate Answers."

4. Klapp's discussion contains some valuable insights, but it also obscures some important issues. For example, whether social typing is accurate and beneficial depends on where a person "is sitting." Klapp notes in his discussion of professionalization (1972:21) that white Anglo-Saxon Protestant males are preferred as physicians. He then happily concludes that "social typing thus helps fit the right person to the right job." Any person who is not a WASP male but wants to be a physician may not be so grateful for this function of social typing. Similarly, Klapp notes that social types help control protest by effecting status degradation ("Red," "Pinko," "Angry Young Man"). It is, of course, a value judgment to say that these effects are beneficial. For the person being degraded, the application of a social label like "Red" or "insane" can be disastrous. Klapp's analysis, then, participates in the "eufunctional" tradition of sociology, which tends to view all change and dissent as bad and to view everything that preserves the status quo as good (Nagel 1961:532; Hempel 1959:297).

5. It is quite possible that contrast conceptions may tend to set the "upper" and "lower" limits for behavioral traits. For example, the images contained in factor 3 and the patient data suggest that a person may be considered crazy if he shows "too much" or "too little" of a particular trait. A person should not be violent, but he should also not be passive and withdrawn; he should cope with "reality" and protect himself, but he should not be "paranoid" and suspicious. The images of violent aggression or passive withdrawal, of manic generosity or paranoid suspicion, apparently set the limits on either end of a behavioral trait. They define what is too much and what is too little and thus define what is proper or improper behavior for the individual.

6. Gove (1975a, 1975b) argues that the rejection and stigma suffered by mental patients are not nearly so severe as labeling theorists claim. A recent study of attitudes toward the mentally ill does not support Gove's argument. Olmsted and Durham (1976) compared data from matched samples of college students from 1962 and 1971. The groups' responses were remarkably similar. Both showed intensely negative attitudes toward the mentally ill (though the 1971 group showed more acceptance of "Ex-Mental Patients" than the 1962 group). The authors concluded that their findings tended to substantiate earlier studies

(Nunnally 1961; Cumming and Cumming 1957). Negative attitudes toward the mentally ill seem to be part of a stable cultural belief system that is not easily altered.

The case of Senator Eagleton also demonstrates that the label "mentally ill" can still carry considerable stigma. This man's political career suffered disastrously merely because he admitted he had been treated with shock for depression. Other sources confirm that former mental patients are stigmatized. Aviram and Segal (1973) have shown that former mental patients are socially rejected and isolated in "ghettos" after discharge, and Greenblatt (1974) has argued that the community's fear and rejection of mental patients are a major force in preventing the phasing-out of mental hospitals.

7. The fifth function mentioned by Klapp is that of status modification. When people begin to view an individual in terms of a social type, his status may be modified—for better or worse. The stereotypes of insanity, of course, are negative and can serve only to degrade a person's status. Once a person is publicly labeled "mentally ill," virtually any of his actions, past or present, can be seen as symptomatic. Or, actions of his that were unequivocally normal can be seen as a "mask," which, until the time of the person's "detection," served only to conceal his essential sickness (Goffman 1961:375; Garfinkel 1956). Stereotypes (and diagnostic labels) can thus generally serve to transform a normal citizen into an "insane person"—a person who is not responsible for his actions and is incapable of making decisions about his own welfare. Klapp's argument notwithstanding, it is the distortion inherent in the stereotypes of insanity that makes this transformation possible. As Nunnally (1961) has shown, the mass media continually characterize the mentally ill as violent, glassy-eyed, catatonic, or laughing maniacally. This image persists even though it has long been established that the behavior of the mentally ill does not generally conform to these stereotypes. These distorted images, however, allow the public to think of the insane as something less than human; and when someone is viewed in this way, he can be treated accordingly. Thus, the stereotypes of insanity may aid in the status degradation of persons labeled "mentally ill," and they also help to justify the treatment of these persons. This point will be discussed in more detail in chapters 3 and 4; see also note 6, above.

Chapter 4

1. In a paper delivered at the American Psychiatric Association convention, Strauss et al.. (1977) presented the results of a highly sophisticated statistical analysis of diagnostic validity and reliability. Their results showed that, although archetypal psychiatric symptoms do exist in patient populations, the great majority of symptoms are much less severe and distinctive. Furthermore, in contrast to symptoms, the great majority of first-admission patients do not group according to the basic syndromes (and ambulatory patients do so even less). The authors conclude that the diagnostician dealing with real patients is forced to place patients in discrete categories of distinctive severe symptoms, even though most patients exhibit low levels of rather ambiguous and mixed symptoms. Present diagnostic categories and procedures simply do not fit the actual nature of the population, and this fact contributes to diagnostic unreliability.

References Cited

Akiskal, H. S., and W. T. McKinney, Jr.
  1973   Depressive Disorders: Toward a Unified Hypothesis. Science 182:20–29.
American Psychiatric Association
  1968   Diagnostic and Statistical Manual. 2d ed. Washington, D.C.: American Psychiatric Association.
Arensberg, C. M., and A. H. Niehoff
  1975   American Cultural Values. In The Nacirema: Readings on American Culture. J. Spradley and M. Rynkiewich, eds. Boston: Little, Brown.
Aviram, U., and S. Segal
  1973   Exclusion of the Mentally Ill. Archives of General Psychiatry 29:126-31.
Bardach, Eugene
  1972   The Skill Factor in Politics: Repealing the Mental Commitment Laws in California. Berkeley: University of California Press.
Barton, Russell
  1959   Institutional Neurosis. Bristol: John Wright & Sons.
Beach, Frank A.
  1955   The Descent of Instinct. Psychological Review 62:401–10.
Bell, G. M.
  1955   A Mental Hospital with Open Doors. International Journal of Social Psychiatry 1:42.
Benedict, Ruth
  1934   Anthropology and the Abnormal. Journal of General Psychology 10:59–80.
Bleuler, Eugen
  1950   Dementia Praecox or the Group of Schizophrenias. J. Zinkin, trans. New York: International Universities.
Bowers, M. B.
  1974   Retreat from Sanity: The Structure of Emerging Psychosis. New York: Human Sciences Press.
Braginsky, B. M., D. Braginsky, and K. Ring
  1969   Methods of Madness: The Mental Hospital as a Last Resort. New York: Holt, Rinehart & Winston.
Braginsky, B. M., M. Grosse, and K. Ring
  1966   Controlling Outcomes through Impression Management:

An Experimental Study of the Manipulative Tactics of Mental Patients. Journal of Consulting Psychology 30:295–300.

Braginsky, B. M., J. D. Holzberg, L. Finison, and K. Ring
1967   Correlates of the Mental Patient's Acquisition of Hospital Information. Journal of Personality 35:323–42.

Breitenstein, Rolf
1968   Der hässliche Deutsche? Munich: Kurt Desch.

Brigham, J. C.
1971   Ethnic Stereotypes. Psychological Bulletin 76:15–38.

Brown, Barbara B.
1974   New Mind, New Body: Biofeedback: New Directions for the Mind. New York: Harper & Row.

Cain, Albert C.
1964   On the Meaning of "Playing Crazy" in Borderline Children. Psychiatry 27:278–89.

Cannon, Walter B.
1942   "Voodoo" Death. American Anthropologist 44:169–81.

Carpenter, W. T., T. H. McGlashan, and J. Strauss
1977   The Treatment of Acute Schizophrenia without Drugs: An Investigation of Some Current Assumptions. American Journal of Psychiatry 134:14–20.

Chauncey, Robert
1975   Comment on "The Labelling Theory of Mental Illness." American Sociological Review 40:248–52.

Ciba Foundation Symposium
1965   Transcultural Psychiatry. Boston: Little, Brown.

Cohen, E. S., H. T. Harbin, and M. J. Wright
1975   Some Considerations in the Formulation of Psychiatric Diagnoses. Journal of Nervous and Mental Disease 160:422–27.

Conolly, John
1856   Treatment of the Insane without Mechanical Restraints. London: Smith Elder.

Cooper, J. E., R. E., Kendell, B. J. Gurland, N. Sartorious, and T. Farkas
1969   Cross-national Study of Diagnosis of the Mental Disorders: Some Results from the First Comparative Investigation. American Journal of Psychiatry 125:21–29.

Cumming, E., and J. Cumming
1957   Closed Ranks: An Experiment in Mental Health Education. Cambridge, Mass.: Harvard University Press.

Davis, A. E., S. Dinitz, and B. Pasamanick
1972   The Prevention of Hospitalization in Schizophrenia: Five Years after an Experimental Program. American Journal of Orthopsychiatry 42:375–88.

Davis, J. M.
1975   Overview: Maintenance Therapy in Psychiatry: I. Schizophrenia. American Journal of Psychiatry 132:1237–45.

139   References Cited

Dinitz, S., M. Lefton, S. Angrist, and B. Pasamanick
    1961   Psychiatric and Social Attributes as Predictors of Case Outcome in Mental Hospitalization. Social Problems 8:322–28.

Dohrenwend, B. P.
    1975   Sociocultural and Social-Psychological Factors in the Genesis of Mental Disorders. Journal of Health and Social Behavior 16:365–92.

Draguns, J., and L. Phillips
    1972   Culture and Psychopathology: The Quest for a Relationship. Morristown, N.J.: General Learning.

Eaton, J. W., and R. J. Weil
    1967   The Mental Health of the Hutterites. In Mental Illness and Social Processes. Thomas J. Scheff, ed. Pp. 92–101. New York: Harper & Row.

Ecker, A.
    1954   Emotional Stress before Strokes: A Preliminary Report of Twenty Cases. Annals of Internal Medicine 40:49–56.

Edgerton, Robert B.
    1966   Conceptions of Psychosis in Four East African Societies. American Anthropologist 68:408–25.
    1969   On the "Recognition" of Mental Illness. In Changing Perspectives in Mental Illness. S. C. Plog and R. B. Edgerton, eds. Pp. 49–72. New York: Holt, Rinehart & Winston.

Engel, G. L.
    1977   The Need for a New Medical Model: A Challenge for Biomedicine. Science 196:129–36.

Feldman, S.
    1974   Community Mental Health Centers: A Decade Later. International Journal of Mental Health. 3(2–3):18–34.

Fogelson, R. D.
    1965   Psychological Theories of Windigo "Psychosis" and a Preliminary Application of a Model's Approach. In Context and Meaning in Cultural Anthropology. M. Spiro, ed. New York: Free Press.

Fontana, A. F., and E. B. Klein
    1968   Presentation of Self in Mental Illness. Journal of Clinical and Consulting Psychology 32:110–19.

Forster, E. B.
    1962   Theory and Practice of Psychiatry in Ghana. American Journal of Psychotherapy 16:7–51.

Fottrell, E., and J. Majumder
    1975   What To Do with the Long-Stay Psychiatric Patient? A Review of a Hundred Cases. Social Psychiatry 10(2):57–61.

Foucault, M.
    1965   Madness and Civilization: A History of Insanity in the Age of Reason. Tr. Richard Howard. New York: Pantheon.

Gardos, G., and J. Cole
  1976   Maintenance Antipsychotropic Therapy: Is the Cure Worse Than the Disease? American Journal of Psychiatry 133:32–36.
Garfinkel, Harold
  1956   Conditions of Successful Degradation Ceremonies. American Journal of Sociology 61:420–24.
Gittelman, M.
  1974   Coordinating Mental Health Systems: A National and International Perspective. American Journal of Public Health 64:496–500.
Goffman, Erving
  1959   The Presentation of Self in Everyday Life. New York: Anchor.
  1961   Asylums. New York: Anchor.
Goldman, A. R., R. H. Bohr, and T. A. Steinberg
  1970   On Posing as Mental Patients: Reminiscences and Recommendations. Professional Psychology 2:427–34.
Gottesfeld, H.
  1976   Alternatives to Psychiatric Hospitalization. Community Mental Health Review 1(1):1–10.
Gove, Walter R., ed.
  1975a   The Labelling of Deviance: Evaluating a Perspective. New York: Wiley.
Gove, W. R.
  1975b   The Labelling Theory of Mental Illness: A Reply to Scheff. American Sociological Review 40:242–48.
Gove, W. R., and T. Fain
  1973   The Stigma of Mental Hospitalization: An Attempt to Evaluate Its Consequences. Archives of General Psychiatry 28:495–500.
Gove, W., and P. Howell
  1974   Individual Resources and Mental Hospitalization: A Comparison and Evaluation of the Societal Reaction and Psychiatric Perspectives. American Sociological Review 39:86–100.
Greenblatt, M.
  1974   Historical Forces Affecting the Closing of Mental Hospitals. Proceedings of a Conference on the Closing of Mental Hospitals. Stanford Research Institute. Pp. 3–17.
Greenley, J. R.
  1972   The Psychiatric Patient's Family and Length of Hospitalization. Journal of Health and Social Behavior 13:25–37.
Greenstein, Fred
  1965   Personality and Political Socialization: The Theory of Authoritarian and Democratic Characters. In Political Socialization: Its Role in the Political Process. Annals of the American Academy of Political and Social Science 361:81–95.

Gruenberg, E. M.
  1967   The Social Breakdown Syndrome—Some Origins. American Journal of Psychiatry 123:12–20.
Gruenberg, E. M., and J. Zusman
  1964   The Natural History of Schizophrenia. International Psychiatry Clinics 1:699.
Gurland, B. J., J. L. Fleiss, J. E. Cooper, R. E. Kendell, and R. Simon
  1969   Cross-national Study of Diagnosis of the Mental Disorders: Some Comparisons of Diagnostic Criteria from the First Investigation. American Journal of Psychiatry 125:30–38.
Hempel, Carl
  1959   Logic of Functional Analysis. In Symposium on Sociological Theory. L. Gross, ed. Evanston, Ill: Row, Peterson.
Hemprich, R. D., and K. P. Kisker
  1968   Die "Herren der Klinik" und die Patienten. Der Nervenarzt no. 39, 10:433–41.
Henry, Jules
  1963   Culture against Man. New York: Random House.
  1965   Pathways to Madness. New York: Random House.
Hoff, Hans, and O. H. Arnold
  1961   Germany and Austria. In Contemporary European Psychiatry. Leopold Bellak, ed. New York: Grove.
Hollingshead, August B., and Frederick Redlich
  1958   Social Class and Mental Illness. New York: John Wiley & Sons.
Honigfeld, G., and R. Gillis
  1967   The Role of Institutionalization in the Natural History of Schizophrenia. Diseases of the Nervous System 28:660–63.
Hsu, F. L. K.
  1972   American Core Value and National Character. In Psychological Anthropology. F. L. K. Hsu, ed. San Francisco: Schenkman.
Jaeckel, Martin, and Stefan Wieser
  1970   Das Bild des Geisteskranken in der Öffentlichkeit. Stuttgart: Georg Thieme Verlag.
Joint Commission on Mental Illness and Health
  1961   Action for Mental Health. New York: Basic Books.
Jones, Maxwell
  1953   The Therapeutic Community. New York: Basic Books.
Kallman, Franz
  1953   Heredity in Health and Mental Disorder. New York: Norton.
Katz, M. M., J. O. Cole, and H. A. Lowery
  1969   Studies of the Diagnostic Process: The Influence of Symptom Perception, Past Experience, and Ethnic Background on Diagnostic Decisions. American Journal of Psychiatry 125:109–19.

Kendell, R. E., J. Cooper, A. Gourley, and J. Copeland
1971   Diagnostic Criteria of American and British Psychiatrists. Archives of General Psychiatry 25:123–30.

Kety, S. S.
1974   From Rationalization to Reason. American Journal of Psychiatry 131:957–63.

Kety, S. S., D. Rosenthal, P. H. Wender, and F. Schulsinger
1971   Mental Illness in the Biological and Adoptive Families of Adopted Schizophrenics. American Journal of Psychiatry 128:302–6.

Kiev, Ari
1972   Transcultural Psychiatry. New York: Free Press.

Klapp, Orrin E.
1972   Heroes, Villains, and Fools. San Diego: Aegis.

Kraepelin, Emil
1902   Clinical Psychiatry. A. Ross Defendorf, ed. New York: Macmillan.

Kringlen, Einar
1969   Schizophrenia in Twins. Schizophrenia Bulletin, December 1969. National Clearinghouse for Mental Health Information.

Kuhn, Manfred, and Thomas S. McPartland
1954   An Empirical Investigation of Self-attitudes. American Sociological Review 19:68–76.

Laing, R. D.
1967   Politics of Experience. Harmondsworth, Eng.: Penguin.

Laing, R. D., and A. Esterson
1964   Sanity, Madness, and the Family. London: Tavistock.

Lambo, T. A.
1964   Patterns of Psychiatric Care in Developing African Countries. In Magic, Faith, and Healing. Ari Kiev, ed. Glencoe, Ill.: Free Press.
1965   Schizophrenia and Borderline States. In Ciba Foundation Symposium: Transcultural Psychiatry. Boston: Little, Brown.

Lamy, R. E.
1966   Social Consequences of Mental Illness. Journal of Consulting Psychology 30:450–55.

Lehrman, Daniel S.
1970   Semantic and Conceptual Issues in the Nature-Nurture Problem. In The Development and Evolution of Behavior. L. Aronson and E. Tobach, eds. Pp. 17–53. New York: Freeman.

Levinson, D. J., and E. B. Gallagher
1964   Patienthood in the Mental Hospital. Boston: Houghton-Mifflin.

Levitz, L. S., and L. P. Ullman
1969   Manipulation of Indications of Disturbed Thinking in

Normal Subjects. Journal of Consulting and Clinical Psychology 33:633–41.

Lindesmith, Alfred, and Anselm Strauss
1950   A Critique of Culture and Personality Writings. American Sociological Review. 15:587–600.

Linton, Ralph
1936   The Study of Man. New York: Appleton-Century-Crofts.
1956   Culture and Mental Disorders. Springfield, Ill.: Charles C. Thomas.

Lippmann, Walter
1930   Public Opinion. New York: Macmillan.

Lipset, S. M.
1961   A Changing American Character? In Culture and Social Character: The Work of David Riesman Reviewed. S. M. Lipset and L. Lowenthal, eds. Glencoe, Ill.: Free Press.

Lowie, R. H.
1954   Toward Understanding Germany. Chicago: University of Chicago Press.

Madsen, W.
1974   The American Alcoholic: The Nature-Nurture Controversy in Alcoholic Research and Therapy. Springfield, Ill.: Charles C. Thomas.

Martin, D. V.
1955   Institutionalization. Lancet 2:1188–90.

Mead, Margaret
1954   The Swaddling Hypothesis: Its Reception. American Anthropologist 56:395–409.
1968   Male and Female. New York: Dell.

Mechanic, David
1972   Response Factors in Illness. In Patients, Physicians, and Illness. E. G. Jaco, ed. New York: Free Press.

Mednick, Sarnoff A.
1970   Breakdown in Individuals at High Risk for Schizophrenia: Possible Predispositional Factors. Mental Hygiene 54:50–63.

Meehl, P. E.
1962   Schizotaxia, Schizotypy, Schizophrenia. American Psychologist 17:827–38.

Milgram, Stanley
1965   Some Conditions of Obedience and Disobedience to Authority. Human Relations 18:57–76.

Miller, D. H.
1961   Psycho-social Factors in the Aetiology of Disturbed Behaviour. British Journal of Medical Psychology 34:43–52.

Miller, Dorothy
1965   Worlds That Fail: Retrospective Analysis of Mental Patients' Careers, Part I. California Mental Health Research Monograph, No. 6.

144 References Cited

1967   Retrospective Analysis of Posthospital Mental Patients' Worlds. Journal of Health and Social Behavior 8:136–40.

Millon, T.
1975   Reflections on Rosenhan's "On Being Sane in Insane Places." Journal of Abnormal Psychology 84:456–61.

Mosher, L. R., W. Pollin, and J. R. Stabenau
1971   Identical Twins Discordant for Schizophrenia: Neurologic Findings. Archives of General Psychiatry 24:422–30.

Murphy, Jane M.
1976   Psychiatric Labeling in Cross-Cultural Perspective. Science 191:1019–28.

Nagel, Ernest
1961   Structure of Science. New York: Harcourt, Brace.

National Institute of Mental Health
1971   Special Report: Schizophrenia. Washington, D.C.: U.S. Government Printing Office.

Newman, Philip L.
1964   "Wild Man" Behavior in a New Guinea Highlands Community. American Anthropologist 66:1–19.

Nunnally, Jum C.
1961   Popular Conceptions of Mental Health. New York: Holt, Rinehart & Winston.

Olmsted, D., and K. Durham
1976   Stability of Mental Health Attitudes: A Semantic Differential Study. Journal of Health and Social Behavior 17(1):35–44.

Orne, M. T.
1962   On the Social Psychology of the Psychological Experiment: With Particular Reference to the Demand Characteristics and Their Implications. American Psychologist 17:776–83.

Osgood, C. E.
1969   Semantic Differential Technique in the Comparative Study of Cultures. In Semantic Differential Technique. C. E. Osgood and James Snider, eds. Chicago: Aldine.

Parsons, Talcott
1951   The Social System. Glencoe, Ill.: Free Press.

Pasamanick, B., F. Scaroitti, and S. Dinitz
1967   Schizophrenics in the Community. New York: Appleton.

Paul, Gordon L.
1969   The Chronic Mental Patient: Current Status—Future Directions. Psychological Bulletin 71:81–94.

Pinel, Phillipe
1962   A Treatise on Insanity. D. D. Davis, trans. New York: Hafner.

Pollin, William
1965   The Use of Discordant Identical Twins in Studies of Schizophrenia. Lecture Presented at Hillside Hospital, 10 November 1965.

Price, R. H.
    1973   The Case for Impression Management in Schizophrenia:
            Another Look. In The Making of a Mental Patient. R. H.
            Price and B. Denner, eds. Pp. 262–75. New York: Holt,
            Rinehart & Winston.
Rawnsley, K.
    1967   An International Diagnostic Exercise. In Proceedings of
            the Fourth World Congress of Psychiatry. Pp. 2683–86.
            Amsterdam: Excerpta Medica Foundation.
Rees, T. P., and M. M. Glatt
    1955   The Organization of a Mental Hospital on the Basis of
            Group Participation. International Journal of Group
            Psychotherapy 5:157.
Riesman, David, with N. Glazer and R. Denney
    1950   The Lonely Crowd. New York: Doubleday-Anchor.
Rimland, Bernard
    1969   Psychogenesis vs. Biogenesis: The Issues and the Evi-
            dence. In Changing Perspectives in Mental Illness. S. Plog
            and R. Edgerton, eds. New York: Holt, Rinehart & Win-
            ston.
Robbins, Lewis L.
    1966   A Historical Review of the Classification of Behavior Dis-
            orders and One Current Perspective. In The Classification
            of Behavior Disorders. Leonard D. Eron, ed. Chicago:
            Aldine.
Rogler, L., and A. Hollingshead
    1965   Trapped: Families and Schizophrenia. New York: Wiley.
Rokeach, M.
    1964   The Three Christs of Ypsilanti. New York: Knopf.
Rosenbaum, Gerald
    1969   Schizophrenia as a "Put-On." Journal of Consulting and
            Clinical Psychology 33:642–45.
Rosenhan, D. L.
    1973   On Being Sane in Insane Places. Science 179:250–58.
    1975   The Contextual Nature of Psychiatric Diagnosis. Journal
            of Abnormal Psychology 84(5):462–74.
Rosenthal, David
    1961   Problems of Sampling and Diagnosis in the Major Twin
            Studies of Schizophrenia. Journal of Psychiatric Research
            1:116–34.
Rosenthal, Robert, and Lenore F. Jacobson
    1968   Teacher Expectations for the Disadvantaged. Scientific
            American 218:19–23.
Sarbin, T. R.
    1954   Role Theory. In Handbook of Social Psychology, Vol. 1,
            first edition. G. Lindzey, ed. Reading, Mass.: Addison-
            Wesley.
    1969   The Scientific Status of the Mental Illness Metaphor. In
            Changing Perspectives in Mental Illness. S. C. Plog and

R. B. Edgerton, eds. New York: Holt, Rinehart & Winston.

Sarbin, T. R., and V. L. Allen
1968   Role Theory. In Handbook of Social Psychology, Vol. 1, second edition. G. Lindzey, ed. Reading Mass.: Addison-Wesley.

Scheff, Thomas
1966   Being Mentally Ill. Chicago: Aldine.
1967   Mental Illness and Social Processes. New York: Harper & Row.
1974   The Labelling Theory of Mental Illness. American Sociological Review 39:444–52.
1975   A Reply to Chauncey and Gove. American Sociological Review 40:252–57.

Schooler, Carmi, and William Caudill
1964   Symptomatology in Japanese and American Schizophrenics. Ethnology 3:172–78.

Shiloh, Ailon
1971   Sanctuary or Prison—Responses to Life in a Mental Hospital. In Total Institutions. S. E. Wallace, ed. Chicago: Aldine.

Siegler, Miriam, and Humphrey Osmond
1974   Models of Madness, Models of Medicine. New York: Macmillan.

Sommer, R., and G. Witney
1961   The Chain of Chronicity. American Journal of Psychiatry 118:111–17.

Spitzer, R. L.
1975   On Pseudoscience, Logic in Remission, and Psychiatric Diagnoses: A Critique of Rosenhan's "On Being Sane in Insane Places." Journal of Abnormal Psychology 84:442–52.

Stanton, Alfred H., and Morris S. Schwartz
1949   Medical Opinion and the Social Context in the Mental Hospital. Psychiatry 12:243–49.

Star, S. A.
1955   The Public's Ideas about Mental Illness. Paper presented to the Annual Meeting of the National Association for Mental Health. Indianapolis, 5 November 1955.

Steadman, H. J., and J. Cocozza
1972   Careers of the Criminally Insane. Lexington, Mass.: Heath.

Stearns, A. W., and A. D. Ullman
1949   One Thousand Unsuccessful Careers. American Journal of Psychiatry 11:801–9.

Strauss, J. S., and W. T. Carpenter, Jr.
1972   The Prediction of Outcome in Schizophrenia. I: Characteristics of Outcome. Archives of General Psychiatry 27:739–46.

Strauss, J. S., et al.
1977   Do Psychiatric Patients Fit Their Diagnoses? Patterns of

Symptomatology as Described with the Biplot. Paper presented at the 1977 meeting of the American Psychiatric Association, Toronto, Canada.

Szasz, Thomas
1960   The Myth of Mental Illness. American Psychologist 15:113–18.
1963   Law, Liberty, and Psychiatry. New York: Macmillan.
1970   The Manufacture of Madness. New York: Harper & Row.
1975   Ceremonial Chemistry: The Ritual Persecution of Drugs, Addicts, and Pushers. New York: Doubleday.

Talbott, J. A.
1974   Stop the Revolving Door—A Study of Readmissions to a State Hospital. Psychiatric Quarterly 48(2):159–67.

Taube, C., and R. Redick
1973   Utilization of Mental Health Resources by Persons Diagnosed with Schizophrenia. Rockville, Md., Biometry Branch, National Institute of Mental Health.

de Tocqueville, Alexis
1901   Democracy in America. Tr. H. Reeve. New York: Appleton.

Townsend, J. M.
1972   Cultural Conceptions and Mental Illness: A Controlled Comparison of Germany and America. Unpublished dissertation. University of California, Santa Barbara.

Tuke, Samuel
1813   Description of the Retreat. York, Eng.: W. Alexander.

Ullmann, L. P., and L. Krasner
1969   A Psychological Approach to Abnormal Behavior. Englewood Cliffs, N.J.: Prentice-Hall.

Vonnegut, Mark
1974   Why I Want to Bite R. D. Laing. Harpers, vol. 248, no. 1487, April, 1974.

Wallace, Anthony F. C.
1972   Mental Illness, Biology, and Culture. In Psychological Anthropology, F. L. K. Hsu, ed. San Francisco: Schenkman.

Wallace, R. K., and H. Benson
1972   The Physiology of Meditation. Scientific American 226:84–90.

Weiner, B.
1975   "On Being Sane in Insane Places": A Process (Attributional) Analysis and Critique. Journal of Abnormal Psychology 84:433–41.

Wing, J. K.
1962   Institutionalism in Mental Hospitals. British Journal of Social and Clinical Psychology 1:38–51.

Yap, P. M.
1951   Mental Diseases Peculiar to Certain Cultures: A Survey of Comparative Psychiatry. Journal of Mental Science 97:313–27.
1965   Phenomenology of Affective Disorder in Chinese and

Other Cultures. In Ciba Foundation Symposium: Transcultural Psychiatry. Boston: Little, Brown.

Yarrow, M. R., C. G. Schwartz, H. S. Murphy, and L. C. Deasy
  1955   The Psychological Meaning of Mental Illness in the Family. Journal of Social Issues 11:12–24.

Zborowski, M.
  1952   Cultural Components in Responses to Pain. Journal of Social Issues 8:16–30.

Zimbardo, Philip
  1972   Pathology of Imprisonment. Society 9:4–8.

Zung, William W.
  1969   A Cross-cultural Survey of Symptoms in Depression. American Journal of Psychiatry 126:116–21.

Zusman, Jack
  1973   Some Explanations of the Changing Appearance of Psychotic Patients. In The Making of a Mental Patient. R. Price and B. Denner, eds. New York: Holt, Rinehart & Winston.

Index